ACTIVITY ANALYSIS
AND THE THEORY OF ECONOMIC
EQUILIBRIUM

ACTIVITY ANALYSIS

AND THE THEORY OF
ECONOMIC EQUILIBRIUM

BY

H. MAKOWER

LONDON

MACMILLAN & CO LTD

NEW YORK · ST MARTIN'S PRESS

1957

HB
171
,M32

MACMILLAN AND COMPANY LIMITED
London Bombay Calcutta Madras Melbourne

THE MACMILLAN COMPANY OF CANADA LIMITED
Toronto

ST MARTIN'S PRESS INC
New York

PRINTED IN GREAT BRITAIN

FOREWORD

THE idea of writing this book I owe to Dr. George Morton. A large part of the work contained in it is his. He has co-operated with me at all stages with infinite patience. If the book would not have been written without his help, it would not have been published without that of Professor L. C. Robbins. His repeated readings, detailed criticism, and constant encouragement have produced whatever degree of coherence the text may now possess. I am very much indebted to Mrs. Land for her exceedingly helpful criticism and to Mr. K. Lancaster for checking through all the algebra and geometry and furnishing certain proofs. Professor R. G. D. Allen made some valuable suggestions. Finally I would emphasize that most of the technique of activity analysis, which may be unfamiliar to some readers in this country, is taken from the work of the Cowles Commission and other writers in the United States.

While I have drawn heavily on many people in writing this book, the responsibility for it is solely my own.

PREFACE

ACROSS the Atlantic several of the leading economists of the day are devoting much of their energies to a new development in economics called activity analysis. The newness of the development lies not so much in its economic content, as in the method of formulating the economic data and handling the solution of economic problems. The use of this new approach is still comparatively recent, and the available literature on the subject is decidedly of a research character, writers cutting their way through to conclusions by the use of the most efficient tool available and for the benefit of their co-researchers, rather than attempting to explain their procedures to spectators on the side-line. Add to this the fact that elementary algebra is essential to the method, and advanced mathematics apparently well suited to it, and it is not surprising that the non-mathematical economists, at least in this country, know very little about what is happening in this field. This, at any rate, is the position of the present writer. I have been looking for a bridge which would link up the important findings of the mathematical pioneers of activity analysis with the economic concepts, principles, and problems with which we non-mathematical economists are familiar. I have found no such bridge, and the gap which separates me from the mathematical economists working on activity analysis is so wide as to disqualify me at the outset from reporting what is being done on the the other side. In spite of this fact I harbour an obstinate conviction that an opportunity is being wasted, a powerful tool of analysis neglected, in favour of the blunter, old-fashioned ones to which we are accustomed. Since I have found no one who has brought down to my level the findings of the mathematically equipped economists in this field, I have attempted to build up a construction of my own. I have tried to see how far the traditional tools of analysis of pure theory could be replaced by a much more explicit and rigidly defined formulation of the production function, the consumption function, and the scarce prime factors. In doing this I have borrowed freely from the works of the writers on activity analysis. But what is presented here is not put forward as a non-technical translation of their findings. I am in no position to give this. Neither am I aiming at it. For one thing, much of the work in question is directed towards 'operational economic planning' or the formulation of the principles of optimal utilization of scarce means in such terms, and for such limited projects, as can be given quantitative empirical content in an actual factory, or on an actual railway system. That this should become possible is highly desirable; and it is one of the main points through which I would seek to justify the present attempt to re-formulate the pure theory of value in the manner presented below that it could, ultimately, give to our economic principles an empirical content. But my work stops far short of this: I remain in the realm of the pure theory of production and consumption and the equilibrium quantities and prices of an abstract economy. Neither is the book confined throughout to the concepts of activity analysis — in Chapter VIII, for instance, some use is made of old-fashioned geometrical constructions.

What are, then, the advantages which the 'activity' approach appears to offer over the traditional approach? What are the limitations of this new approach, and what are the pitfalls?

The first advantage is clarity. In the method of formulation used here every element of the system is explicit. Every relationship between variables is, if not at once obvious, at least definitely traceable. If we are to put a stop to the interminable cross-purpose debates over the workings of incompletely specified models, it seems essential that we should state in full the system of relationships postulated, and, furthermore, that we should cease working with general functions such as $P = f(L,C)$ ('quantity produced is some function of labour and capital input') and substitute specific functions both for production and for consumption. The functions used here, both for production and consumption, are linear in terms of the inputs (a discussion of this point will be found in Chapter VI). But the point I wish to emphasize here is only that the use of specific functions prevents a vast amount of misunderstanding so common in economic literature.

Moreover, if we can enunciate our economic principles by reference to a system in which all the elements are explicit and the relationships clear, we at least have principles which are *capable*, in principle, of being interpreted in terms of real things in an actual factory. As I have already said, this book nowhere goes beyond pure theory — some of it supremely abstract. But it aims at a theory which is cast in such a form that it could be translated into actual technical processes of production in a factory or actual patterns of deployment of a fleet of buses.

The third advantage which appears to me to derive from the activity formulation is that it is applicable to the analysis of large changes in the data. Its validity is not confined to infinitely small or small variations. I believe that this is important. Many problems, including most problems relevant to economic policies, involve sizable changes, not small ones. We are not interested in the effect of an infinitely small depreciation of the pound sterling, or of an infinitely small increase in the income tax. The use of the infinitesimal calculus as a tool of analysis seems to have an undue hold here; there are (I am told) other mathematical techniques. I think it is a considerable advantage of the activity formulation that it implies kinked curves, not smooth ones, that it throws into relief the limitational factors of the system, by showing a sharp change when the equilibrium turns over from one set of limitational factors to another. The calculus approach teaches us to focus our attention upon the rates of substitution 'in the neighbourhood of equilibrium'. But in equilibrium the substitution rates in production are all equal to those in consumption, and in point of exposition this equality is a drawback, not an aid. It is altogether easier for the ordinary person to think in terms of discrete rather than infinitesimal changes.

In working with this formulation I have found that it has a way of exposing flaws in the accepted body of economic doctrine. Many of these are, of course, well understood; but whether already known or unknown they are shown up when the old tissue of economic doctrine is stretched out upon this new mechanical loom. I have tried to suggest why an attempt to re-express basic economic theory in terms of this new approach is worth while. But the proof of the pudding is in the eating. I am putting forward only a tool of analysis, no new findings. Whether it is worth doing depends upon whether it enables the reader to cut more quickly through to the heart of economic problems, to check more certainly upon economic arguments, to arrive more quickly and reliably at solutions.

What are the limits of the new approach? I am very uncertain. But two points need making: first, unresolved conundra at the basis of our economic reasoning cannot be solved simply by putting them into the new machine. The main relevant case in point is the problem of maximizing the utility of a group of people. I do not see how this can be done on the basis of economic reasoning. And unless and until a meaning can be given to the concept of social welfare, we cannot give general solutions to problems of optimal allocation in a community. This is one of the two reasons why in the following pages a far more complete treatment will be found of the Crusoe economy than of community economies. Indeed I would make the point more broadly: I think that this formulation can clarify moot points in economic theory, but cannot spirit away basic deficiencies in that theory.

Second, there is one limitation which I have found very restricting. It is that I have found no sufficiently manageable way of embodying into the activity formulation exchange within the system. Thus no theory of exchange as such will be found. And topics such as the theory of taxation are presented in activity form only under exceptionally rarefied abstract conditions, in order to circumvent the deficiency.

I would conclude with a warning. The whole art in using this tool lies in setting it. You have to find *how* to represent the data of any particular problem. There is not one way, there are dozens of different ways in which one can draw up activity tables. Any complete tabulation, any matrix with the necessary constraints, will start churning out some answer. The very inexorableness of its workings tends to make us accept the answer as true. And it is always a true answer — but to what question? The crucial and fallible point in this, as in any other method of approach, lies right at the beginning in the formulation of the problem. One formulation will constitute a valid analogue to the economic problem under consideration, another will not. Human fallibility at this initial stage of the building of the model has as much scope in this as in any other form of analysis, even though I believe that the scope for error in subsequent stages is much reduced.

In publishing this material my hope is that it will quickly be judged obsolete rather than irrelevant. Surely there is something to be got by non-mathematical economists from activity analysis, and surely there is someone equipped to give it to us ?

CONTENTS

xiv   *Contents*

PART 1

OPTIMAL ALLOCATION OF RESOURCES IN A CRUSOE ECONOMY

CHAPTER I

THE PROBLEM

The Technology of Production

THE Theory of Equilibrium consists in the analysis of production, tastes, and the equilibrium prices and quantities which tend to be set up through the interaction of these two basic sets of data. The traditional method of presenting this analysis seems to suffer from two sorts of weakness. First, the analysis of production is largely implicit and is more vague than is necessary (the analysis of tastes is still more vague, but this is due to the inherent limitations of economics in respect of psychological phenomena). Second, excessive attention is paid to the symptoms of equilibrium, at the expense of an adequate presentation of the underlying processes by which it is established. More specifically, economists appear to be fascinated by the fact that, under certain assumptions about the relevant functions, it is a feature of equilibrium that the marginal rate of substitution between any pair of goods should be the same in production and in consumption. What the mechanism is whereby this equality is reached is often left pretty vague in the mind of the student. Yet it is this mechanism of allocating resources optimally, and not the symptom of equality of the marginal rates, which is important. And the subject of efficient allocation of resources is broader than, independent of, and in a way prior to the problem of the equilibrium allocation. Students are often drilled in the art of representing geometrically the equilibrium quantities and prices of two commodities which can be produced in varying combinations (according to a concave 'production opportunity function') and in respect of which the consumer has a certain system of preference (convex indifference curves). The emphasis is laid upon the fact that the equilibrium must fall at a point of equal slope on the production function and the consumption function. But nothing is said about how the producer arrives on his 'production opportunity curve'. He may easily not do so. It is the main task of production management to seek to come as near to this boundary as possible. This is true in every enterprise — whether undertaken by a business, a government, a military leader, or an explorer. Of course, in all these cases we need to know the goal in view, which is set by the demand side. This determines what part of the boundary to go for.

What is needed is a form of analysis which spells out the technically efficient methods of reaching a given goal, and exposes to view the processes by which the goal itself is 'given' by the interaction of demand conditions and production conditions. It is this aspect of the analysis which needs more emphasis in economic theory teaching. And the analysis is particularly important because it has a *practical* bearing. Up till recently there has been really no way in which the economist could connect his cost functions with the activities of the business man. Yet this is a waste of information : the real content of the cost function is technological. It is capable of precise and, in principle, quantitative formulation. Such a formulation is not only possible for the economist to achieve ; it can be of use to the business man when he has achieved it. In any complex concern, such as, for instance, I.C.I., it is not obvious, but, on the contrary, exceedingly difficult to see, without the aid of a systematic formulation of production conditions, what is the most efficient way of utilizing the vast number of different resources to produce the complex pattern of final goods. A whole range of alternative arrangements is open, in regard to the places of production of all the outputs, the technical methods used, the materials, the timing. Business men conducting complex concerns of this sort might welcome a systematic routine for computing minimum costs in such cases. And, more certainly, unless economists can formulate their production analysis in terms which have an empirical meaning in production activities, business men will have little use for economists' analysis. In other words, the economist should formulate his analysis of production in terms of real production activities, defined in terms of the men, machinery, materials, and techniques used. He should show the distinction between efficient and inefficient patterns of activities, and between those which are well adapted and those which are ill-adapted to demand.

If the formulation is to be capable of application in actual enterprises, the production function must be given a specific form, not merely expressed in a general form. It is not sufficient to say that the output of wheat is 'some function' of the acreage of land and the number of man-hours and machine-hours used for its production. We have to say *what* function. And we have to specify this for each method or process of production which is or might be used. To put it the other way round, the production processes between which the entrepreneur is choosing must all be translated into precise functions. To select functions which fit or reflect the actual technology of an industry is to some extent an art, and what is 'the best fit' in any instance will remain a matter of debate even among experts. But there is one question of general interest : should the functions chosen to depict technology be linear, or should non-linear functions be used ? It seems to the present writer that those who are proceeding with the use of linear equations to depict production activities have chosen the right path, for two reasons : first, if we really specify all the factors affecting output in a given activity, then there would appear to be no source of non-linearity in the function relating input of factors with output of products. This may be contested on the ground that we cannot, and should not, include in our analysis all factors relevant to output, and that we must therefore be able to deal with the general case of non-proportionality between inputs and outputs. If this view be accepted, the use of linear equations might still be justified on the ground that even where, in terms of the variables included in the analysis, a production function is non-linear, we can approximate it as closely as we like by a series of linear relationships. This will be preferable because it is easier to handle, and because in practical life most people find it easier to think in terms of discrete variations, rather than continuous functions. The whole question of the interpretation of 'variable returns' is examined in more detail in Chapter VI. For the present we proceed with our linear relationships.

We have come then to the conclusion that value analysis should be based on the production side upon the technology of production ; that this should be represented explicitly by the use of specific input-output relationships ; and that linear relationships should be employed.

The 'Technology' of Tastes

If this approach is adopted for the analysis of production, we shall have to follow it also in handling demand. It seems to us that as regards the demand side there is no strong case either for or against depicting tastes by a set of linear equations relating consumer goods to consumer satisfaction. From one point of view it might be said that the utility functions can as well be left vague : since as economists we know very little about the 'technology of consumption' — the way in which satisfaction may be influenced by varying the patterns of consumer goods — there is nothing lost, no information thrown away, by failing to render these relationships specific. But any form of equilibrium analysis must assume the existence of *some* sort of function on the tastes side; and — since we can approximate any non-linear relationship as closely as we please by the use of a series of linear ones — we lose nothing, beg no new question, by depicting tastes, as well as production, through a set of specific linear relationships. This is what has been done in the following analysis. We shall consider further the implications of this at a later stage; but the reader is warned at the outset that the extension of activity analysis to cover the demand as well as the supply side of value theory, although foreseen and written about by economists several years ago, is here pushed further than in the accepted literature of activity analysis. For we are here going to present equilibrium theory as such, the conjunction of supply and demand, and the resulting equilibrium quantities and 'values' of goods, in terms of activity analysis.

A Lacuna : No Theory of Exchange

One final point : to some people the theory of equilibrium may signify a theory of market values, including a theory of the exchange of goods between different individuals. This is not what is presented here. Our analysis contributes nothing to the theory of exchange itself, it tells us nothing about either so-called 'competitive behaviour' or monopolistic behaviour. The presentation we use here analyses resources and the structure of supply on the one hand and demand on the other. It tells us how equilibrium quantities and values result from the interaction of these, and how they vary under certain variations in data. It covers completely, in principle, the problems of a unified or Crusoe economy. In so far as it is applied — and we shall thus apply it — to problems of the real world which involve exchange between a multiplicity of individuals, it begs or takes for granted the solution of the problems of market behaviour. Since we shall be very largely concerned with closed economies, as constrasted with open economies and partial equilibrium analysis, we shall be exhibiting the same weakness here as traditional expositions of economic theory. For there is surely no satisfactory theory of market behaviour in general equilibrium analysis.

Throughout the text we shall give more attention to the analysis of supply than to that of demand, to the structure of production than to that of consumption. This is simply because there is more that an economist can say about the former than about the latter. But demand conditions still constitute an integral part of the equilibrium problem and its solution; we have always to incorporate the assumed conditions of demand, even if we do not discuss them.

In accordance with the above paragraphs, we seek to present our analysis of production in terms of all the various different technical processes of production, or production activities, which can be undertaken with *given prime resources*. The analysis must reveal which is the optimal way of utilizing any given set of prime resources, i.e. the way which secures the greatest possible value of output. The analysis must show which of the various technically possible activities are efficient; which of these should, given the demand conditions, be carried on at all; at what level each of them should be carried on, and how much of each final commodity will be obtained.

Before trying to give any sort of systematic formulation of the equilibrium problem along these lines, we give in the remaining paragraphs of this chapter some very simple examples of the production problem handled in terms of explicit techniques or processes and, introducing assumed demand conditions, we give the solutions to these element- ary problems.

Production Management in Farming

Suppose that there is a farmer who has at his disposal 400 man-weeks of labour and 2000 acres of land and that he is considering whether to go in for sheep farming or arable farming. He might know that 10 sheep valued at £100 could be raised for every 200 acres and 5 man-weeks devoted to the sheep. Arable farming may be carried on by more intensive or less intensive methods. Suppose the farmer considers just two alternative methods of arable cultivation: an extensive method using much land and rather little labour and a more intensive method which requires less land but more labour. For example, 10 tons of grain worth £100 might be produced either on 100 acres with 50 man-weeks or on 80 acres with 60 man-weeks.

We can summarize the position as follows:

	RESOURCES REQUIRED PER £100 OUTPUT			RESOURCES AVAILABLE
	SHEEP FARMING	GRAIN GROWING		
		EXTENSIVE	INTENSIVE	
	I	II	III	
Labour (man-weeks)	5	50	60	400
Land (acres)	200	100	80	2000
Output (£)	100	100	100	

TABLE 1

We seek to find the greatest amount of money that can be earned on the farm, and how it can be earned. The amount that could be earned by concentrating wholly on sheep farming is $10 \times £100 = £1000$, since the resources (400 man-weeks and 2000 acres) are sufficient for 10 'lots' of 5 man-weeks plus 200 acres.[1] Here the effective limit to production is set by the supply of land.

If all resources were concentrated on extensive grain growing the maximum number of 'lots' of 50 man-weeks plus 100 acres is 8 and the maximum value of the total crop would be £800. Here the effective limit to output is set by the total labour supply. Finally, if resources are concentrated entirely upon intensive cultivation of grain the number of 'lots' is limited to 6·67. This limit is set again by the labour supply; for there would be enough land for 25 lots. With 6·67 lots of factors the total value of output if resources are invested in intensive grain cultivation is £667.

Of the three alternatives considered, sheep farming is the most profitable; but the most profitable arrangement of all is not achieved by turning the whole farm over to sheep farming since this would leave most of the labour — 350 man-weeks — unused. It is profitable to devote some resources to grain because a small contraction of sheep farming activities (below the maximum) will release sufficient land to enable good use to be made of the 350 idle man-weeks of labour. For example, if only 1800 acres of land are allocated to sheep grazing, the value of sheep raised drops from £1000 to £900; but the release of 200 acres would enable the farmer to draw idle labour into the cultivation of the land; on extensive methods 200 acres would enable him to grow grain to the value of £200 (using 100 of the idle man-weeks). Thus mixed farming

[1] 400 man-weeks could furnish as many as 80 teams of 5 men working for a week. But 2000 acres will provide only 10 plots of 200 acres. Therefore, since men without land cannot produce any sheep, there is a maximum of 10 'lots' of 5 men with 200 acres. Since each such lot produces £100 of sheep, the maximum return which the farmer could get if he concentrated wholly on sheep farming is £1000.

is going to be more profitable than sheep farming alone. In the present simple case total money earnings are maximized by so combining sheep raising and extensive grain growing that both of the prime resources — land and labour — are exactly used up. If the farmer were to transfer 600 acres of land out of sheep farming into intensive grain cultivation, this would require 450 man-weeks of labour as against a total of 400 man-weeks of labour available. By transferring from sheep raising to *extensive* arable farming, the labour supply can be made to go further. 600 acres here require only 300 man-weeks. But now we are near the profitable proportion of arable farming. Another 100 acres, bringing the total to 700, would raise the amount of labour needed in grain growing to 350; and 800 acres would require, even on extensive farming, the total labour that is available (400 man-weeks) leaving none for sheep farming. By trying out the figures between 700 and 800 in extensive grain farming we find that the total labour and land available is approximately used up, and the total value of output maximized, by allocating 737 acres of land in extensive grain farming. The final picture is then as follows :

	SHEEP FARMING	EXTENSIVE GRAIN FARMING	INTENSIVE GRAIN FARMING	TOTAL
Man-weeks	$31\frac{1}{2}$	$368\frac{1}{2}$	nil	400
Acres	1262	737		1999
Output ($£$)	631	737		1368

TABLE 2

As compared with the output of $£$1000 obtainable from pure sheep farming, the best pattern of mixed farming yields $£$1368. This is possible because of a fuller utilization of resources, eliminating the waste of labour involved in pure sheep farming.

Allocation of Resources in Transport Networks

The problem of finding the optimum allocation of resources confronts every enterprise — from a business deploying its resources of men, materials, and finances to a polar expedition utilizing the rigidly fixed resources which they unload from the ship on to the ice. It stands out particularly clearly in any transport or communication enterprise. Professor Koopmans has used shipping to work out some of the principles of activity analysis, and we shall look at a very simple example of his shipping problem.

Suppose that there are four ports: Hull, Plymouth, Dieppe, and Dublin. Suppose that a shipping company has 2 boats at Dieppe and 6 at Dublin. Suppose further that there are no cargoes at these ports, but that there are cargoes for 3 boats at Hull and for 5 at Plymouth. What is the best way to re-deploy the idle boats? We may take as a measure of the cost incurred the number of days that any boat sails in ballast. Suppose that the sailing times are as follows:

Dieppe to Plymouth	2 days
Dublin to Plymouth	3 „
Dieppe to Hull	4 „
Dublin to Hull	6 „

Would it be best to send the Dieppe boats to Plymouth? Or to Hull? Or some to both? Where should the Dublin boats be sent? In other words, which routing of the empty ships will minimize the total number of ship-days spent in switching the 2 ships at Dieppe and the 6 ships at Dublin to Plymouth and Hull, 5 being required at Plymouth and 3 at Hull?

We can write all the information down in summary form:

	No. of Boats required at Hull	Plymouth
	3	5
No. of Boats available at		
Dieppe 2	(4 days)	(2 days)
Dublin 6	(6 days)	(3 days)

The travelling times between each pair of ports are written in brackets in the appropriate box — for instance, Dublin to Plymouth takes 3 days.

Now in this example we can quickly reckon the costs of every possible alternative, because only three alternatives are open, given that we have to furnish 3 boats at Hull and 5 at Plymouth. For let us start by supposing that we put both the Dieppe boats on the Plymouth run. Then there is only one possible way of utilizing the rest of the shipping. Because if Dieppe boats are put on the Plymouth run this means that no Dieppe boats can be put on the Hull run. This in turn means that all 5 boats for Hull must be sent from Dublin, and that the 6th Dublin boat must be sent to Plymouth. To summarize:

	Hull	Plymouth
Required at	3	5
Dieppe ships sent to	0	2
∴ No. of Dublin ships that must be sent to	$3-0=3$	$5-2=3$

Similarly, if we put both Dieppe ships on the Hull run we have:

	Hull	Plymouth
Required at	3	5
Dieppe ships sent to	2	0
∴ No. of Dublin ships that must be sent to	$3-2=1$	$5-0=5$

Finally, if we put 1 Dieppe ship on the Hull run and 1 on the Plymouth run we have:

	Hull	Plymouth
Required at	3	5
Dieppe ships sent to	1	1
∴ No. of Dublin ships that must be sent to	$3-1=2$	$5-1=4$

No other way of fulfilling the requirements exists. The total cost — which is measured by the total number of

ship-days spent in shifting the fleet to where it is wanted —
of each of the three alternative methods of deployment is
given by simply multiplying the number of boats on any
run by the number of days that run takes.

Thus on the first alternative we have:

	On Hull Run	On Plymouth Run	Total
Ship-days spent by Dieppe boats	0	$2 \times 2 = 4$	4
,,　　,,　　Dublin　,,	$3 \times 6 = 18$	$3 \times 3 = 9$	27

Grand Total :　31

On the second alternative we have:

	On Hull Run	On Plymouth Run	Total
Ship-days spent by Dieppe boats	$2 \times 4 = 8$	0	8
,,　　,,　　Dublin　,,	$1 \times 6 = 6$	$5 \times 3 = 15$	21

Grand Total :　29

On the third alternative we have:

	On Hull Run	On Plymouth Run	Total
Ship-days spent by Dieppe boats	$1 \times 4 = 4$	$1 \times 2 = 2$	6
,,　　,,　　Dublin　,,	$2 \times 6 = 12$	$4 \times 3 = 12$	24

Grand Total :　30

Thus the cheapest routing is to put both the Dieppe
boats on the Hull run — implying that 1 Dublin boat is
put on the Hull run, and 5 on the Plymouth run.

This answer has been quickly obtained simply by
trying out every possible alternative. But if even one more
port is added, the number of alternatives increases greatly.
Suppose the ships in Ireland are located in 2 ports — 3
ships being in the north and 3 in the south of Ireland.
Then instead of 3 possible ways of moving the required
number of ships to Plymouth and Hull, there are 9.

Obviously if we imagine a quite ordinary shipping company, it may have ships in many more than 3 ports, and it may need to move them to many ports, instead of 2. And, further, any degree of complexity may be introduced by the fact that the number at any one port is not generally fixed, but rather there are freights of varying profitability at different ports; and similarly the number of empty ships at each port is not fixed, but can be varied by incurring certain costs.

We shall not try to solve any of these complex cases here. Our principal object at this stage is rather to present the problem of optimum arrangement of production resources in terms which are suitable for the approach we wish to use.

International Allocation of Resources

One other important allocation problem may be cited: that of international specialization. Here again the fundamental feature of optimal production is the adaptation of production activities to the fixed supplies of prime resources in each country. World production is increased if each country specializes in those production processes for which its resources are particularly suitable; the desired consumption patterns may then be reached by trading.[1] If in the example of the farm (pp. 9-11) the ownership is divided, one owner having $31\frac{1}{2}$ man-weeks and 1263 acres, the other $368\frac{1}{2}$ man-weeks and 737 acres, the first could produce

---

[1] It is commonly said that international trade brings gain owing to the fact that it *permits* the international division of labour. The matter might be more clearly expressed by saying that international trade brings gain because it enables the world to *adapt* optimally to the international division of land, machinery, and all other limited resources, including labour. For labour and other resources *are* divided internationally, somewhat rigidly, and the question at stake is whether the optimum set of production activities to fit these given resources in each place can be utilized — as is true under free trade — or whether this optimum set cannot be chosen because of barriers to trade.

approximately 63 sheep and the second approximately 74 tons of grain. This is the same total production as under a single owner, and provided the two owners are free to exchange their produce, they could each have the same consumption pattern as before — i.e. consumption in the ratio $\frac{14}{13}$ tons of grain to 1 sheep. If, however, no exchange of produce is possible and consumers wish to maintain this consumption ratio, each owner must produce the two products in the specified ratio. In this case total production would fall to approximately 32 sheep and 34 tons of grain, the first owner being able to put only a fraction of his land to use, and the second having idle labour.

Geometrical Representation of an Allocation Problem

For the above three sample problems we have arrived at approximate solutions by a process of trial and error.

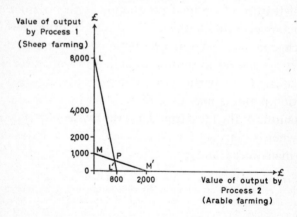

FIG. 1

Graphical methods may also be useful. Thus the farm problem is depicted in Fig. 1. Along the vertical axis of a system of Cartesian co-ordinates is measured the value of output produced by Process I (sheep farming). Along the horizontal axis is measured the value of output produced by Process II (arable farming). If nothing is produced by Process II, labour would suffice to produce $\frac{400}{5} \times 100 =$

£8000 by Process I. This gives the point L with co-ordinates (0,8000). On the other hand, if nothing is produced by Process I, labour would suffice to produce $\frac{400}{50} \times 100 = £800$ by Process II. This gives L′ with co-ordinates (800,0). Any combination of outputs from the two processes which lies on the line LL′ requires just as much as the total labour supply. Points inside the line will require less than the total supply, and points outside it would require more than the total labour supply.

Labour, however, is not the only factor required. We must also demarcate the zone of output combinations for which the total available land supply suffices. Thus the point M on the vertical axis measures the maximum amount of output from Process I for which the land supply would suffice, if nothing were produced by Process II (co-ordinates 0,1000; for $\frac{2000}{200} \times 100 = £1000$). Similarly point M′ shows the maximum output using Process II for which land would suffice (co-ordinates 2000,0; for $\frac{2000}{100} \times 100 = £2000$). Any combination of outputs from Processes I and II which lie on or inside the line MM′ is feasible from the point of view of land supply.

Only those output combinations for which there is enough land *and* enough labour are possible. That is, only outputs which are on or within both lines LL′ and MM′ (i.e. on or within the bent line MPL′) are feasible. Points inside this boundary are never optimal; the maximum output will be either at the point (P) of intersection of LL′ and MM′ or else (if both LL′ and MM′ have a slope greater than −1) at L′ or (if both slopes are less than −1) at M.   In the present example the optimal outputs of sheep and grain respectively are £631 worth of sheep and £737 worth of grain.

CHAPTER II

OPTIMAL ALLOCATION OF RESOURCES:
THE FORMAL REPRESENTATION IN
A SIMPLIFIED MODEL

Formulation of the Farm Production Problem

IN the preceding chapter we have instanced a few exceedingly simple production problems, framing them in terms
of the alternative input-output combinations or technical
processes which are available to the entrepreneur. We
gave the solutions to these problems, but these we reached
by common sense and without any systematic routine for
finding them. The problems we are dealing with in the
foregoing and the present chapter are so simple that their
formalization and systematic handling is indeed in itself
not only unnecessary but tedious. The only excuse for it
is that we are feeling our way step by step to the more
general equilibrium problem where a systematic approach
is far from superfluous. We want therefore to find a
more systematic procedure so that it can be applied to
more complex problems not amenable to solution by
common sense.

Let us consider again the farming problem of Chapter I.
Here the technical processes of production are represented
by the columns of figures showing inputs and outputs:
an input of 5 man-weeks and 200 acres is associated
with an output of 10 sheep (valued through demand
conditions at £100). This constitutes the only technique

of sheep production. Then an input of 50 man-weeks and 100 acres produces 10 tons of grain (also valued at £100). This constitutes one technique or process of grain growing. Finally an input of 60 man-weeks and 80 acres also produces 10 tons of grain, representing an alternative productive process in grain growing. Each of these input-output relations is a technical process or *production activity*. It is in the nature of such an activity that it can be carried on at any level — high or low — without any change in the input-output relationship which constitutes the activity. In other words, whether only 5 man-weeks and 200 acres are used, or 5000 man-weeks and 200,000 acres, the output per unit of the (composite) input is always unchanged — 10 sheep in the first case, and 10 in the second. Thus constant returns to *the scale of each production activity* are embodied in this representation.

So much for the technological data. We must also incorporate the limitations on available productive resources. We need only specify the primary resources: these, taken with the technological processes for producing intermediate products, depict the whole of the data on the production side. In the example in Chapter I there is in effect only a single type of end-product, which is money: so long as the relative price of sheep and grain is taken as fixed, we can eliminate reference to these individual products and treat the problem simply as that of finding the optimum way of allocating the limited labour and land between three different technical processes all producing money. In this case the sole criterion of good and bad allocation of resources is found in the total quantity of money obtained, so that we simply have to find, from the production data, how to maximize money receipts, and no representation of data about consumers' preferences for meat and grain is necessary; it has been subsumed in the money prices. In this very reduced form, the solution to the problem is made to depend solely on the production data.

In finding the optimum allocation of resources between sheep farming and arable farming (p. 9), two conditions must be fulfilled: first, the production plan cannot be such as to prescribe, for any one particular productive activity, proportions between the different inputs and outputs other than those dictated by the technical conditions governing that line. In other words, technological conditions must be taken into account. Second, the production plan cannot be such as to utilize, over all the productive activities together, more of any productive resource than is available. In other words, the limitation of prime resources must be taken into account. We can choose from a variety of plans within these conditions. The problem is to maximize total output *subject* to these two types of restriction.

The first restriction means that *the production arrangement must be such as to provide, in any given production activity, for precisely that proportion between all the inputs and outputs which is needed by (and indeed defines) that particular production activity*. Extensive grain farming, in our example, uses 50 man-weeks and 100 acres per £100 worth of grain. There is no varying the set of ratios 50 : 100 : 100 *in extensive grain growing*. If we contemplate using a smaller acreage with more labour, this represents a variation of the production method itself — from extensive to intensive arable farming. Thus the first condition to which we have to conform is that the production arrangement must be such as to provide, in each given production activity, for precisely that set of ratios of all the inputs and outputs which prevails in this activity.

This leaves open a whole range of possible production arrangements: one could put all one's effort into intensive grain growing, or all into sheep raising, or one could do mixed farming, concentrating more or less on one or other line. But now we have to take into account the second kind of condition under which we are planning our production : *the production arrangement cannot be such as to utilize, over all the productive activities together, more of any resource than is available.*

We may write down the production conditions for sheep and extensive grain farming compactly as follows :

	ACTIVITIES		RESOURCES
	PRODUCTION		
	I	II	
Intensities	x_1	x_2	
Man-weeks	5	50	400 man-weeks
Acres	200	100	2000 acres
Value of output	100	100	Max.

TABLE 3

If we consider these figures column-wise, they give us the first restriction : a column gives us a set of fixed ratios — the set which must be used in that particular line of production. If we consider the figures row-wise, *in conjunction with* the scale upon which each activity is being carried on, they give us the second restriction : a row of figures, each multiplied by the scale of the activity, gives (by summing) the total amount of a factor which will be used up.

The units chosen for quoting factors and outputs in Table 3 are arbitrary. We can, of course, rewrite the figures to express the quantities of factors needed per £1 of output instead of per £100, the figures in columns I and II being now divided by 100. Further, we can change the unit of accounting for labour and land, and quote labour in units of 400 man-weeks and land in units of 2000 acres, the first row of figures being divided by 400, and the second row by 2000. Thus our figures become:

$\dfrac{5}{100} \div 400$	$\dfrac{50}{100} \div 400$	1 labour unit or
$\dfrac{200}{100} \div 2000$	$\dfrac{100}{100} \div 2000$	1 land unit
£1	£1	

(a)

$\dfrac{25}{200,000}$	$\dfrac{250}{200,000}$
$\dfrac{200}{200,000}$	$\dfrac{100}{200,000}$
1	1

(b)

TABLE 4

For convenience this 'normalized' form is used below.

Formal Representation of a Two-Process Enterprise, assuming Linear Relationships

In order to depict any production problem of the same nature as the farming example, we shall replace the figures by symbols. We shall confine ourselves in the present chapter to economies with only two activities, two inputs and a uniform output.

We then have, for this type of problem:

	ACTIVITIES		RESOURCES
	I	II	
Input 1	a_{11}	a_{12}	1
Input 2	a_{21}	a_{22}	1
Output	1	1	

TABLE 5

Now whatever the actual values of the a-coefficients are, there are only three sub-cases that need be studied in order to get a quick method of finding the best possible production arrangement for all problems of this simple type — that is, with only two production activities, two joint inputs and a uniform output.

Sub-case 1 arises where one column shows smaller figures for both rows than does the other column, e.g. :

ACTIVITIES		RESOURCES
I	II	
7	2	I
5	3	I
I	I	

TABLE 6

This would mean that one production activity or production process uses less of both labour and land than the other process.

It is immediately obvious that the process which uses less of both factors is the only process that should be used. (All resources would be used on Process II, and total output would be $\frac{1}{3}$ in the above example.)

Sub-case 2 arises where one row shows lower figures in both columns than does the other row, e.g.

ACTIVITIES		RESOURCES
I	II	
7	5	I
2	3	I
I	I	

TABLE 7

This would mean that one factor of production effectively limits the output both when Process I is used and when Process II is used.

It is immediately obvious that the limiting factor is the decisive one, and that resources will be devoted wholly to whichever process requires less of the limiting factor. (In the example, the first factor is limiting under both processes. Process II requires less of this factor than

Process I. Process II will be used exclusively, and total output will be $\frac{1}{5}$.)

These two sub-cases are very easily answered by common sense; we should not need all this apparatus if production conditions always conformed to one or other of them.

Sub-case 3. This is the case when neither of the above situations prevails. One column is not consistently smaller than another; nor is one row consistently smaller than another. That is, in the notation of Table 5 above,

$$a_{11}, a_{22} > a_{12}, a_{21} \text{ or } a_{11}, a_{22} < a_{12}, a_{21}.$$

Finding the best allocation of resources in this type of situation, extended, of course, to many more than two production activities and many more than two factors of production, constitutes the central job of production management. In the highly simple case of two activities, two factors and a uniform product to which we confine ourselves in this chapter, the optimum allocation is easily found. Assuming that we are able to allocate any fraction of labour, with the appropriate fraction of land, to either process, that is that both factors are perfectly divisible, it is in this case possible and advantageous to make the allocation such as to leave no resource idle. Thus to find the best production arrangement in this situation we find that allocation of resources which utilizes all resources. We did this previously by trial and error. We can do it more quickly by elementary algebra.

Let the level of activity in Process I be x_1
,, ,, ,, II ,, x_2.

Then the total amount of labour used is $a_{11}x_1 + a_{12}x_2$.

And the total amount of land used is $a_{21}x_1 + a_{22}x_2$.

Further, the total amount of labour available is 1,
and ,, ,, land ,, 1.

So that, in order to leave no resources, we must make each of these expressions equal to 1:

$$a_{11}x_1 + a_{12}x_2 = 1 \qquad . \qquad . \qquad . \qquad (1)$$

$$a_{21}x_1 + a_{22}x_2 = 1 \qquad . \qquad . \qquad . \qquad (2)$$

$$\therefore \; x_1 = \frac{1 - a_{12}x_2}{a_{11}} \qquad . \qquad . \qquad . \qquad (3)$$

Substituting for x_1 in equation (2) we get:

$$x_2 = \frac{a_{21} - a_{11}}{a_{12}a_{21} - a_{11}a_{22}} \qquad . \qquad . \qquad (4)$$

If we consider only the first two activities of the farming example set out above (p. 9) we may apply these new formulae to find the optimal allocation of resources on the farm.

Here $a_{11} = \dfrac{25}{200,000}$, $a_{12} = \dfrac{250}{200,000}$, $a_{21} = \dfrac{200}{200,000}$, $a_{22} = \dfrac{100}{200,000}$ (and we have $25 < 250$; $200 > 100$; $25 < 200$; $250 > 100$).

Applying equations (3) and (4):

$$x_2 = 200,000 \left(\frac{200 - 25}{200 \times 250 - 100 \times 25} \right) = 736 \cdot 84.$$

and

$$x_1 = 200,000 \left(\frac{1}{25} \right) - \frac{250}{25} \times 736 \cdot 84 = 631 \cdot 6.$$

From the optimal division of output between Processes I and II the optimal allocation of each factor of production follows directly.

For on Process I we require $\dfrac{25}{200,000}$ labour units of 400 man-weeks to produce £1, that is, $\dfrac{25}{200,000} \times 631 \cdot 6$ labour units of 400 man-weeks to produce £631·6. The total labour allocated to Process I should therefore be 31·58 man-weeks.

On Process II we require $\dfrac{250}{200,000}$ labour units of 400 man-weeks to produce £1, that is, $\dfrac{250}{200,000} \times 736.84$ units of 400 man-weeks to produce £736.84. The total labour allocated to Process II should therefore be 368.42 man-weeks.

Similarly on Process I we require $\dfrac{200}{200,000}$ land units of 2000 acres to produce £1, that is, $\dfrac{200}{200,000} \times 631.6$ land units of 2000 acres to produce £631.6. Total land allocated to Process I should therefore be 1263.2 acres.

On Process II we require $\dfrac{100}{200,000}$ land units of 2000 acres to produce £1, that is, $\dfrac{100}{200,000} \times 736.84$ land units of 2000 acres to produce £736.84. Total land allocated to Process II should therefore be 736.84 acres.

This is the algebraic system behind the results we reached less accurately in Chapter I (p. 11).

The Role and Representation of Consumption

In the whole analysis so far we have assumed that the different commodities produced have *fixed relative prices* (i.e. one sheep always sells for the same quantity of money as one ton of grain). By so doing we have greatly simplified the analysis; in fact, we have in effect evaded the whole problem of multiple consumption, for any set of commodities having fixed relative prices may always be treated as a single commodity. Our analysis is, however, deficient: relative prices are not fixed, but in general variable.

We must therefore develop a technique which enables us to handle cases where the relative prices of commodities, that is, the rates at which the consumer is willing to substitute one for another, are variable — where, in fact, consumer tastes are permitted to play their full role. As a first step towards this end we shall re-formulate our problem in terms of quantities only. There will be no implicit reference to prices — such as appears in the assumption that 5 man-weeks labour with 200 acres produces 10 sheep valued at £100, and 50 man-weeks together with 100 acres produce 10 tons of grain valued at £100. Instead of building into our problem these fixed relative prices of consumer goods, we shall build in *fixed relative quantities* of consumer goods. That is, people consume the goods in a fixed proportion. This does not generalize our analysis. To assume a fixed ratio between the quantities of the goods consumed is neither more nor less general than to assume a fixed ratio between their prices. The advantage in changing over to a formulation of the problem under conditions of fixed relative quantities is rather that such a formulation is free of any reference to prices. All our magnitudes are now in terms of physical quantities. We have, of course, again (as when assuming fixed relative prices of consumer goods) begged a central question in assuming a fixed pattern of consumption. But we use this assumption only as a stepping-stone in our analysis. Once we have found the solution under the assumption of fixed bundles of consumer goods, we shall extend the analysis to the general case where the proportion in which commodities are consumed varies.

Optimal Allocation of Resources with a Rigidly Fixed Consumption Pattern

Consider once more the farmer owning limited resources of land and labour, and seeking to divide them optimally between sheep farming and arable farming. Suppose the technical conditions in each line are as

previously postulated; and suppose further that consumers demand sheep and grain in the ratio 2 sheep to 1 ton
of grain. We may formulate this as follows:

	ACTIVITIES			RESOURCES
	PRODUCTION		CONSUMPTION	
	I	II	III	
Labour	5	50	0	400
Land	200	100	0	2000
Sheep	10	0	20	0
Grain	0	10	10	0
Consumption units	0	0	1	Max.

TABLE 8

Here the third activity is a *consumption* activity. In this
consumption activity the 'inputs' are the outputs of the
production activities — sheep and grain. To get one
bundle constituting a final consumption unit, we have to
put in 20 sheep and 10 tons of grain. The question is:
what allocation of prime resources to Activities I and II
will maximize the number of consumption units?

We shall first solve this problem graphically. Along

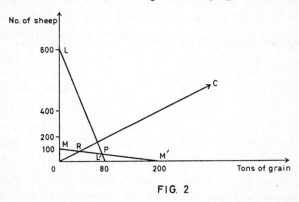

FIG. 2

the vertical axis of a system of Cartesian co-ordinates
measure the number of sheep produced (Fig. 2). Along

the horizontal axis measure the tons of grain produced. Divide the whole area into that part containing all combinations of sheep and grain for which the available supply of labour is sufficient, on the one hand, and the area containing all combinations for which the available labour supply is insufficient, on the other. The boundary making this division is found in the way already explained in Chapter I. Mark on the vertical axis a point L showing the number of sheep for which there is enough labour, assuming all labour goes to sheep farming. Since 5 manweeks produce 10 sheep the total supply of 400 manweeks could produce 800 sheep. The co-ordinates of the point L are (0,800). Similarly, if no sheep are produced labour would suffice for $\frac{400}{50} \times 10 = 80$ tons of grain. This gives a point L' on the horizontal axis, with co-ordinates (80,0). Turning now to the second limitational factor, we can find the dividing boundary for separating those output combinations which are possible from the point of view of land supply from those which are not. This is a straight line joining a point M on the vertical axis with co-ordinates (0,100) and a point M' on the horizontal axis with co-ordinates (200,0) (since if all land were devoted to sheep raising the farmer would get $\frac{2000}{200} \times 10 = 100$ sheep; and if all were devoted to arable he would get $\frac{2000}{100} \times 100 = 200$ tons). So far our construction is very similar to that of Fig. 1, except that we work in physical quantities throughout. We now introduce the consumer bundle containing the fixed proportion 20 : 10, or 2 : 1, as between number of sheep and tons of grain. This is represented by the line OC running through the origin at a slope of 2 : 1.

The assumption that consumers always consume in this fixed ratio means that our solution must lie some-

where along the line OC. Further, it cannot lie outside
the boundary MPL′, and it will not lie inside that boundary,
because this would not maximize consumption. Hence it
will lie on the boundary MPL′, and on the line OC — that
is, the intersection (R) of OC with MPL′ gives the solution,
i.e. the optimal outputs of sheep and of grain. The
determination of these outputs directly determines in turn
the inputs of labour and land into sheep farming and grain
growing.

The algebraic solution of this problem may be obtained as follows. Normalizing the figures in Table 8 with
respect to units (so that labour is quoted in terms of 400
man-weeks, and land in terms of 2000-acre plots), we get:

	ACTIVITIES			RESOURCES
	I	II	III	
Labour	$\dfrac{25}{2000}$	$\dfrac{250}{2000}$	0	1
Land	$\dfrac{200}{2000}$	$\dfrac{100}{2000}$	0	1
Sheep	10	0	20	0
Grain	0	10	10	0
Consumption Units	0	0	1	Max.

TABLE 9

Now let the level of activity in Process I be x_1 (so that
output of sheep is $10x_1$),

and let the level of activity in Process II be x_2 (so that
output of grain is $10x_2$),

and let the level of activity in Process III, i.e. the level of
consumption, be x_3 (representing a consumption of $20x_3$
sheep and $10x_3$ tons of grain).

The conditions of the problem are:

(1) That total amount of labour used in all processes
cannot exceed 1 unit (of 400 man-weeks).

(2) That total amount of land used in all processes cannot exceed 1 unit (of 2000 acres).

(3) That total consumption of sheep cannot exceed total production of sheep.

(4) That total consumption of grain cannot exceed total production of grain.

The problem is to maximize the level of consumption (x_3) subject to these conditions. It is clear that, in the present simple case where outputs are not joint, the consumption of each item should not only not be greater than the production, but should be exactly equal to the production. If production were not arranged in this way, the farmer would be wasting resources on an item which was being thrown away, and therefore he would not be maximizing consumption. It might seem on first thoughts that, in a similar way, for the maximization of consumption we must necessarily use up all labour and all land, rendering conditions (1) and (2) also into equalities instead of inequalities. However, a moment's reflection shows that this is not so : the problem we have selected for examination is one in which inputs of labour and land in production are joint in given proportions, and the inputs of the two products in consumption are joint in a fixed proportion, whereas the outputs of sheep and grain are independent. It may not in general be possible to find an arrangement which exhausts the two factors, or even if possible it may not (given the consumption pattern) be optimal (we shall be concerned with this point further in Chapter III). Given this particular problem of joint inputs, independent outputs and fixed consumption pattern, the maximization of consumption implies that we must exactly use up *one or other* of the two scarce factors, leaving in general a margin of the other one unused. For the fully utilized factor the above condition ((1) or (2)) is changed into an equality, while for the other factor it remains an inequality indicating an unused surplus. We do not know in advance which factor will prove to be the fully utilized one. We therefore try making each factor in turn fully utilized. This gives us two alternative solutions to our problem. It is the *smaller* of these solutions — the one giving the lower value to x_3 the level of consumption — that is the relevant one. This is because a consumption level is feasible only if the scarcity of *both* factors is taken into account. To use the higher value would be to pre-suppose a production arrangement such as that represented by a point in the area MPL or L'PM' in Fig. 2. Such an arrangement is possible from the point of view of *one* factor, but in order to be really possible we must find an arrangement which is possible from the point of view of both factors simultaneously — i.e. we cannot go outside the boundary MPL'. We therefore have either

(1′) Total amount of labour used in all processes = 1

or

(2′) Total amount of land used in all processes = 1.

The conditions which will give the solution are either

$$(1') \quad \frac{25}{2000}x_1 + \frac{250}{2000}x_2 = 1$$

$$(3') \quad 10x_1 = 20x_3$$

$$(4') \quad 10x_2 = 10x_3$$

or

$$(2') \quad \frac{200}{2000}x_1 + \frac{100}{2000}x_2 = 1$$

$$(3') \quad 10x_1 = 20x_3$$

$$(4') \quad 10x_2 = 10x_3.$$

Solving the first three equations first we get:

$$x_1 = 2x_3 \text{ (from (3'))}$$
$$x_2 = x_3 \text{ (from (4'))},$$

and substituting for x_1 and x_2 in equation (1′) we get

$$x_3 = \frac{20}{3}.$$

Solving now the second three equations we get again:

$$x_1 = 2x_3$$
$$x_2 = x_3,$$

and substituting for x_1 and x_2 in equation (2′) we get:

$$x_3 = 4.$$

Since this second value for x_3 is smaller than the first $\left(4 < \dfrac{20}{3}\right)$, it gives us the maximum level of consumption, with $x_3 = 4$, $x_1 = 8$, and $x_2 = 4$.

The optimum production arrangement in terms of *total* inputs and outputs, is therefore as follows:

	ACTIVITIES		
	PRODUCTION		CONSUMPTION
	I	II	III
Labour	$\dfrac{25}{2000} \times 8 = \dfrac{200}{2000}$	$\dfrac{250 \times 4}{2000} = \dfrac{1000}{2000}$	0
Land	$\dfrac{200}{2000} \times 8 = \dfrac{1600}{2000}$	$\dfrac{100 \times 4}{2000} = \dfrac{400}{2000}$	0
Sheep	$10 \times 8 = 80$	0	$20 \times 4 = 80$
Grain	0	$10 \times 4 = 40$	$10 \times 4 = 40$

TABLE 10

Here the factors are still quoted in normalized units, viz.: units of 400 man-weeks, 2000 acres.

Converting back to man-weeks and acres by multiplying labour figures by 400 and land figures by 2000, we get:

	TOTAL INPUTS AND OUTPUTS		
	I	II	III
Labour	40	200	0
Land	1600	400	0
Sheep	80	0	80
Grain	0	40	40
Final consumption bundles	0	0	4

TABLE 11

It is seen that the total land used = 1600 + 400 = 2000 = total supply.

It is seen that the total labour used = 40 + 200 = 240 = less than total supply.

Thus land is fully utilized, and labour is not.

The reader may well be waiting for a demonstration of how the equilibrium solution is found for a more general, interesting case — how would a firm owning a dozen factories in different places, supplying fifty consumer markets distributed throughout the country, and producing half a dozen items under conditions of joint production, best allocate its given resources? That is the kind of case which makes our present approach worth while. Nevertheless, we shall have to disappoint anyone who is hoping to be given here a demonstration of the solution for such general cases. The technique of solution is a fairly lengthy numerical operation — or succession of operations. The most widely used method is known as the Simplex method, and is to be found in the basic works on activity analysis. The reader who is prepared to work through the necessary mathematics is referred to these works.[1] The optimum solution is found by successive trials of the alternatives which are open, and which are indicated by the set of inequalities which constitute the constraints of the matrix. In the general case the number of unknowns is greater than the number of relationships, and it is necessary to find out, by trial, which of the unknowns may be discarded, that is, which activities are not used. Some indication of how this may be done, without having to try out exhaustively all the possibilities open, will be found at the end of Chapter V.

[1] See, for instance, *Activity Analysis of Production and Allocation* (Ed. T. C. Koopmans), chapters xxi and xxii, by G. B. Dantzig. Also Charnes, Cooper, and Henderson, *An Introduction to Linear Programming*.

CHAPTER III

OPTIMAL ALLOCATION OF RESOURCES WITH JOINT INPUTS, JOINT OUTPUTS, AND JOINT DEMAND

Introductory

ONE of the main reasons why we need a more systematic and explicit formulation of the economic data than is vouchsafed in the usual marginal analysis stems from the presence of 'jointness' in the system: jointness between factors in producing a given output, jointness between products derived from a given factor input, and jointness between products in furnishing a given utility to the consumer. If there were no jointness anywhere in the system, the procedure of singling out variables two at a time, and studying the relationship between the pair, would be sufficient. As soon as the property of jointness is recognized — as it must be if we want our analysis to be capable of application to the real world — to be the rule rather than the exception, this approach is insufficient. Economists have tried to meet this difficulty both by insisting that they will conduct their analysis in terms of small, infinitely small, variations in each variable and the impact on the related variables; and by endeavouring *without* any systematic explicit statement of the whole system to 'allow' for 'secondary effects' — by some sort of common-sense hunches. Neither of these devices seems to the author to be acceptable, particularly not if we claim that the object of economic theory is to provide, ultimately, a system of thought for use in real business and real government departments. For practical enterprises are working with known techniques — techniques which are certainly not in general free of 'jointness'. There seems to be no justification for adopting a method of analysis in economic science which ignores an important part of the real data.

In the next three chapters we shall try to re-state the theory of equilibrium quantities and values in a Robinson Crusoe economy under stationary conditions, assuming jointness not only between inputs (as in Chapter II) but between outputs of the production activities, and between inputs of a number of consumption activities as well. In Chapter III we formulate the system in terms of the technologies of production and consumption and establish the conditions of equilibrium. In Chapter IV we shall seek out in this formally complete (though very limited) system the 'marginal productivities' and 'marginal utilities' of familiar text-book economics. We shall still be able to identify them; but the process of so doing will be so complex and tortuous as to raise serious doubts whether these entities provide the best way into an insight into optimum allocation of resources in a real business. In Chapter V we shall proceed from the equilibrium quantities established for Crusoe's economy to derive the equilibrium values (or internal prices — there are no market prices) of the system. We shall show that these are equal to the marginal productivities and the marginal utilities of the used processes derived from first principles in Chapter IV.

An Economy with Joint Inputs, Joint Outputs and Joint Demand

Up to now we have limited our analysis to a model which was really insufficient to demonstrate the mechanism of equilibrium in an economy. On the production side, although we allowed for co-operation between factors in producing a given output, outputs were strictly independent of each other, no wool ever being produced together with mutton.   Furthermore, the number of different production activities allowed into our analysis was limited initially to three, and latterly to only two.   In dealing with only two we were really begging part of the solution to our problem.   For we assumed that we already knew which activities, given the supply of prime resources and the consumer demand, would be the best ones to use.   It is important that it should be understood that the selection of optimal production processes really involves two stages of elimination.   First, from all the conceivable techniques of production we eliminate those which, irrespective of the endowments of prime resources in a particular economy and irrespective of demand, produce less of everything. Thus it is generally possible to think of ways of doing a job which use more labour, more machinery, more time and more materials than the best known method : such ways are *inefficient*.   Suppose then that from the table of all conceivable production activities we have eliminated inefficient activities, there remains the next stage, the selection of those activities which, given the prime resources and the tastes in the economy, should be used.   This is the problem of optimum allocation of resources between efficient activities, so as to maximize utility derived from given resources (or minimize the amount of resources used up in producing a given utility).   In the formulation below we shall assume that inefficient activities have already been eliminated.   But we shall incorporate more efficient activities than those that are used in equilibrium, so as to illustrate the process of selection of optimal activities. We shall also be dealing with activities which produce joint outputs of more than one product (as well as retaining joint inputs from our previous model).

On the demand side we have hitherto begged a central issue in supposing that the pattern of consumption — the relative quantities in which goods are consumed — was given to us as a datum. That is, we considered only one consumption activity. In fact, one of the things which the analysis must enable us to determine is the selection of the equilibrium consumption pattern, out of many possible ones, so as to maximize utility. We can generalize our analysis by supposing that we know only *the set of alternative consumption bundles* which give the same satisfaction to the consumer. In other words, in accordance with established procedure we rest our analysis upon the supposition that the consumer has a definite indifference system, and we embody this into our tabulation of data. Thus we may write down any number of consumption activities, each of which shows a different commodity combination yielding a given utility.

Our formulation of the data of the problem is given in Table 12. General coefficients are used instead of numbers. For clarity, inputs have been distinguished from outputs by inserting a negative sign before the input coefficients. The table shows six production activities and three consumption activities (these numbers are, of course, arbitrary). Outputs from production activities become inputs in consumption activities. In place of the I in columns VII, VIII and IX we might have written a general utility index. The consumption activities in our matrix describe alternative bundles of output yielding a given level of consumer satisfaction. It is not necessary to assume that this is cardinally measurable; we simply denote the given level by the index I.

Now attention should be drawn to an important point which arises when we formulate the consumer preference function in our activity matrix. It is the same point as has already arisen on the production side, but is likely to raise more serious doubts in the context of tastes than in the context of production. Our formulation means that on whatever scale each activity is carried on, the utility derived per unit consumption is the same. Moreover, with the formulation of the economic data as it stands below, we

| | ACTIVITIES | | | | | | | | | RESOUR |
| | PRODUCTION | | | | | | CONSUMPTION | | | |
Intensities	I x_1	II x_2	III x_3	IV x_4	V x_5	VI x_6	VII x_7	VIII x_8	IX x_9	
Input 1	$-a_{11}$	$-a_{12}$	$-a_{13}$	$-a_{14}$	$-a_{15}$	$-a_{16}$	o	o	o	-1 unit Input
Input 2	$-a_{21}$	$-a_{22}$	$-a_{23}$	$-a_{24}$	$-a_{25}$	$-a_{26}$	o	o	o	-1 unit Input
Output 1	a_{31}	a_{32}	a_{33}	a_{34}	a_{35}	a_{36}	$-a_{37}$	$-a_{38}$	$-a_{39}$	o
Output 2	a_{41}	a_{42}	a_{43}	a_{44}	a_{45}	a_{46}	$-a_{47}$	$-a_{48}$	$-a_{49}$	o
Utility	o	o	o	o	o	o	1	1	1	Max.

TABLE 12

shall always have unit income-effect. This point will be taken up in some detail in Chapter VI. It will be shown there that whatever view one may take of the economic content of our constructions, there is no great difficulty about modifying the constrained matrices in such a way that, formally, we provide for all types of diminishing utility and costs. The point at issue here is not a simple one, and readers will be wise to reserve judgment upon it, at any rate until after they have read Chapter VI. Meanwhile, having stated that it is formally quite easy to modify the matrix so as to secure 'diminishing utility', we shall proceed to use the unmodified matrix, which is simpler.

The Equilibrium

Given, then, the formulation of the data as set out in Table 12, how do we deduce from it the equilibrium quantities of factors of production allocated to each productive process and the quantities of consumer goods produced in all these processes and consumed? The number of unknowns which we seek to determine is nine — the scale upon which each of the nine activities is carried on, which also gives us (when multiplied by the appropriate a-coefficients) the amount of resources allocated to each industry and consequently the amounts of output produced in each productive process and consumed.

Now, to solve for the nine unknowns we have four relationships:

(1) That the sum of the inputs of manpower in all activities cannot exceed 1.[1] That is,

$$\sum_{j=1}^{9} a_{1j} \, x_j \leqslant 1.$$

(2) That the sum of the inputs of land in all activities cannot exceed 1.[2] That is,

$$\sum_{j=1}^{9} a_{2j} \, x_j \leqslant 1.$$

(3) That the total quantity of sheep produced equals the total quantity consumed. That is,

$$\sum_{j=1}^{6} a_{3j} \, x_j = \sum_{k=7}^{9} a_{3k} \, x_k.$$

(4) That the total quantity of grain produced equals the total quantity consumed. That is,

$$\sum_{j=1}^{6} a_{4j} \, x_j = \sum_{k=7}^{9} a_{4k} \, x_k.$$

So far we have four relationships (two equations and two inequalities) to solve nine unknowns. We have, however, to take into account the fact that the nine activities, although all efficient, are not necessarily all used in equilibrium. In fact, it can be proven mathematically that the equilibrium solution will never necessitate the use of more than four

---

[1] The unit of labour has been normalized.
[2] The unit of land has been normalized.

activities in an economy which has only four 'commodities', by which we mean factors and consumer goods.

We shall discuss this important and by no means obvious proposition a little further in Chapter X. For the moment we shall take it for granted. It means that there are only four activities which are carried on out of the nine (the 'scale' of production in the other five is zero). Which four activities are used? As already indicated, there is no simple prescription for detecting, in a problem like this, which will be the used activities. Basically this has to be solved by some form of trial and error, to find out which set of four yields the maximum utility, although various short-cut devices have been worked out (as indicated in Chapter V) which reduce the work of trial and error. We shall imagine here that this work has already been done, and that it is known which five activities it is unprofitable to use in equilibrium. Let us say that they are Processes I, IV, V, VI, and IX. To simplify, we drop them out of the matrix. Then we have:

	ACTIVITIES				RESOURCES
	PRODUCTION		CONSUMPTION		
	II	III	VII	VIII	
Intensities	x_2	x_3	x_7	x_8	
Input 1	$-a_{12}$	$-a_{13}$	0	0	-1
Input 2	$-a_{22}$	$-a_{23}$	0	0	-1
Output 1	a_{32}	a_{33}	$-a_{37}$	$-a_{38}$	0
Output 2	a_{42}	a_{43}	$-a_{47}$	$-a_{48}$	0
Utility	0	0	1	1	Max.

TABLE 13

We now have only the four scales of activity or 'intensities', those for Processes II, III, VII, and VIII, to determine. We also have four relationships (p. 41 above). The only question is how to apply the two first, which state that the total amount of each factor used must be 'equal to or less than' the available supply. In the example worked out in Chapter II our data were such that (except in very special cases) only one factor could be fully utilized. In the present more general formulation, where the consumption pattern is variable, it is possible and profitable to use fully all of the limited resources and at the same time to waste none of any product, provided certain conditions prevail. These conditions are: that the ratio of factor endowments should be within the ratios of technical coefficients of inputs in efficient productive activities; and that the ratio of technical coefficients of outputs in efficient production activities should be within the range of ratios of inputs in efficient consumption activities. Given these conditions the optimal allocation of resources will be such as to utilize all of both factors, while producing no excess of either output. In other words both of the first relationships should be taken as equalities, giving

$$a_{12}x_2 + a_{13}x_3 = 1 \qquad . \qquad . \qquad . \qquad (1)$$
$$a_{22}x_2 + a_{23}x_3 = 1 \qquad . \qquad . \qquad . \qquad (2)$$
$$a_{32}x_2 + a_{33}x_3 = a_{37}x_7 + a_{38}x_8 \qquad . \qquad . \qquad (3)$$
$$a_{42}x_2 + a_{43}x_3 = a_{47}x_7 + a_{48}x_8 \qquad . \qquad . \qquad (4)$$

These four equations determine the four levels of activity x_2 x_3 x_7 and x_8. They are:

$$x_2 = \frac{a_{13} - a_{23}}{a_{13}\,a_{22} - a_{12}\,a_{23}},$$

$$x_3 = \frac{a_{22} - a_{12}}{a_{13}\,a_{22} - a_{12}\,a_{23}},$$

$$x_7 = \frac{(a_{13} - a_{23})(a_{42}\,a_{38} - a_{32}\,a_{48}) + (a_{22} - a_{12})(a_{43}\,a_{38} - a_{33}\,a_{48})}{(a_{13}\,a_{22} - a_{12}\,a_{23})(a_{47}\,a_{38} - a_{37}\,a_{48})},$$

$$x_8 = \frac{(a_{13} - a_{23})(a_{42}\,a_{37} - a_{32}\,a_{47}) + (a_{22} - a_{12})(a_{43}\,a_{37} - a_{33}\,a_{47})}{(a_{13}\,a_{22} - a_{12}\,a_{23})(a_{48}\,a_{37} - a_{38}\,a_{47})}.$$

We may then write out the problem of allocation of resources, with its solution, in the following activity matrix, the values of the x's being those just given.

	ACTIVITIES									RESO
	I	II	III	IV	V	VI	VII	VIII	IX	
Intensities	o	x_2	x_3	o	o	o	x_7	x_8	o	
Input 1	$-a_{11}$	$-a_{12}$	$-a_{13}$	$-a_{14}$	$-a_{15}$	$-a_{16}$	o	o	o	-1
Input 2	$-a_{21}$	$-a_{22}$	$-a_{23}$	$-a_{24}$	$-a_{25}$	$-a_{26}$	o	o	o	-1
Output 1	a_{31}	a_{32}	a_{33}	a_{34}	a_{35}	a_{36}	$-a_{37}$	$-a_{38}$	$-a_{39}$	o
Output 2	a_{41}	a_{42}	a_{43}	a_{44}	a_{45}	a_{46}	$-a_{47}$	$-a_{48}$	$-a_{49}$	o
	o	o	o	o	o	o	1	1	1	Ma

TABLE 14

The total amount of resources going into each activity is given by multiplying the intensities (or scale) of each activity into each of the coefficients. These total amounts are written out below in what we may call the Allocation matrix. The x's are, of course, now no longer unknown.

	ACTIVITIES			
	II	III	VII	VIII
Input 1	$-a_{12}x_2$	$-a_{13}x_3$	o	o
Input 2	$-a_{22}x_2$	$-a_{23}x_3$	o	o
Output 1	$a_{32}x_2$	$a_{33}x_3$	$-a_{37}x_7$	$-a_{38}x_8$
Output 2	$a_{42}x_2$	$a_{43}x_3$	$-a_{47}x_7$	$-a_{48}x_8$

TABLE 15

CHAPTER IV

PRODUCTIVITIES AND UTILITIES

The Productivities of Factors of Production

IN order to provide a bridge between the traditional way of presenting value theory and that being used here, it may be helpful at this stage to seek out what, in our present formulation, represents those corner-stones of traditional exposition, marginal productivity and marginal utility. In certain very simple cases this is immediately obvious. Suppose, for instance, that in the data of Tables 12–15 we make $a_{21} = a_{31} = 0$. Then, in the first activity our allocation matrix will show the total quantities:

$$
\begin{array}{ll}
\text{Input 1} & -a_{11}x_1 \\
\text{Input 2} & 0 \\
\text{Output 1} & 0 \\
\text{Output 2} & a_{41}x_1.
\end{array}
$$

If instead of considering the absolute amounts of outputs and inputs we consider the relative amounts, we get $\dfrac{a_{41}}{-a_{11}}$ as the output per unit of Input 1 (which we may call labour). This, obviously enough, is the productivity of Input 1 in Activity 1. If, further, we were to assume that in Activity II $a_{12} = a_{32} = 0$ we should get, similarly, the ratio $\dfrac{a_{42}}{-a_{22}}$ as the productivity of Input 2, say land.

If, however, there is jointness with respect to inputs we are, as is familiar, in the position that the productivity of a factor cannot be determined in a single activity under conditions of fixed technical coefficients. With joint inputs, there is a certain output produced jointly by two or more factors. Knowledge of the amounts of the inputs and of the output *in a single activity* does not enable us to attribute any particular fraction of the total output to an individual factor of production. For in such circumstances factors of production cannot be substituted for each other within a single process. But they can be substituted for each other in the system as a whole, by the substitution of *one activity for another*. To substitute an activity using a high proportion of labour to land for an activity using a low proportion of labour to land, is to substitute labour for land. Suppose that a given output of wheat may be obtained by two different activities as follows :

	I	II
Man-weeks	− 50	− 55
Acres	− 100	− 80
Tons of wheat	100	100

TABLE 16

Here a reduction of 20 acres in the amount of land used in the production of 100 tons of wheat has to be offset by an increase of 5 man-weeks. Thus for any given pair of activities, we can read off the relative productivities (or substitution rates) for any pair of inputs :

$$\frac{\text{difference between land input under the two activities,}}{\text{difference between labour input under the two activities,}}$$

where the unit level of each activity has been so chosen as to equalize outputs. The productivities as thus defined refer to a given pair of production activities. For each such pair there will be a different relative productivity. Thus the relative productivity, i.e. the substitution rate between the factors with respect to any given pair of activities, is given by the ratio :

$$\frac{a_{ij} - a_{ik}}{a_{hk} - a_{hj}}$$

where the first subscript refers to the number of the row in the activity matrix, and the second subscript to the number of the column. This formula applies where there are joint inputs, but no jointness in output.

As soon as there are joint outputs as well as joint inputs, the definition of the productivities becomes very complex. Since, however, the concept is used so much in traditional exposition, it may be worth while following through what it means in terms of the technological data.

Consider, for instance, the following activities :

	II	III
Labour	− 70	− 100
Land	− 200	− 150
Meat	50	65
Grain	190	80

TABLE 17

A switch from Activity III to Activity II, raising the level of activity in the latter by one unit, increases grain in Activity II by 190 and decreases grain in Activity III by more than 80. Instead of the drop of $\frac{7}{10}$ of 80 which would follow from the transfer of 70 units of labour to Activity I, we have to reckon the larger reduction $\left(\frac{200}{150} \times 80\right)$ due to the withdrawal of land.

In more general terms, we may have a matrix :

	ACTIVITIES		
	I	II	III
Input 1 (Labour)	− a_{11}	− a_{12}	− a_{13}
Input 2 (Land)	− a_{21}	− a_{22}	− a_{23}
Output 1	a_{31}	a_{32}	a_{33}
Output 2	a_{41}	a_{42}	a_{43}

TABLE 18

The productivity of labour (Input 1) may be traced as follows. When the level of activity in Activity II is raised by one unit by shifting resources from Activity III, and the total amount of land (Input 2) is kept constant, then :

In Activity II Output 2 is raised by a_{42}.

In Activity III Output 2 falls by $\dfrac{a_{22}}{a_{23}} \cdot a_{43}$.

∴ Total change in Output $2 = a_{42} - \dfrac{a_{22}}{a_{23}} \cdot a_{43}$.

Similarly, change in Output $1 = a_{32} - \dfrac{a_{22}}{a_{23}} \cdot a_{33}$.

Assume that the value of a unit of Output 1 in terms of Output 2 is S. Then the total change in output =

$$\left(a_{42} - \frac{a_{22}}{a_{23}} \cdot a_{43} \right) + S \left(a_{32} - \frac{a_{22}}{a_{23}} \cdot a_{33} \right)$$

Now consider the change in labour accompanying the switch from Activity III to Activity II :

In Activity II labour increases by a_{12}.

In Activity III labour decreases by more than a_{13} because the reduction is governed by the proportionately larger withdrawal of land, so that input of labour falls by $\dfrac{a_{22}}{a_{23}} \cdot a_{13}$. Thus the productivity of labour with respect to Activities II and III is measured by the change in output associated with a switch between Activity III and Activity II divided by the change in labour input associated with this switch. That is, *labour productivity* is measured, for a switch to the less labour-intensive activity, i.e. a decrease in labour, by :

$$\frac{\left(a_{42} - \dfrac{a_{22}}{a_{23}} \cdot a_{43} \right) + S \left(a_{32} - \dfrac{a_{22}}{a_{23}} \cdot a_{33} \right)}{a_{12} - \dfrac{a_{22}}{a_{23}} \cdot a_{13}}$$

or for a switch in the opposite direction, i.e. for an increase in labour, by:

$$\frac{\left(a_{43} - \dfrac{a_{23}}{a_{22}} \cdot a_{42}\right) + S \left(a_{33} - \dfrac{a_{23}}{a_{22}} \cdot a_{32}\right)}{a_{13} - \dfrac{a_{23}}{a_{22}} \cdot a_{12}} \qquad . \quad (1)$$

The two expressions are equal.

To find the productivity of land in respect of Activities II and III, we consider a switch between the activities keeping total labour used constant. Let the level of activity in Activity III rise by one unit at the expense of Activity II.

In Activity III Output 2 rises by a_{43}.

In Activity II Output 2 falls by more than a_{42} because instead of the fall of a_{42} which would accompany the transfer of land to Activity III, we have to reckon the proportionately larger fall due to the transfer of labour, i.e.

In Activity II Output 2 falls by $\dfrac{a_{13}}{a_{12}} \cdot a_{42}$.

Similarly, Output 1 rises in Activity III by a_{33}.

Output 1 falls in Activity II by $\dfrac{a_{13}}{a_{12}} \cdot a_{32}$.

Thus the total change in output =

$$S \left(a_{33} - \frac{a_{13}}{a_{12}} \cdot a_{32}\right) + \left(a_{43} - \frac{a_{13}}{a_{12}} \cdot a_{42}\right).$$

The change in the input of land (Input 2) associated with the switch between Activities II and III is as follows:

In Activity III land increases by a_{23}.

In Activity II land decreases by more than a_{22} because we have to allow for the proportionately larger reduction in labour. Thus in Activity II land decreases by $\dfrac{a_{13}}{a_{12}} \cdot a_{22}$.

Thus the productivity of land in respect to Activities II and III is measured by the change in output associated with a switch between Activity II and Activity III divided by the change in land input associated with this switch. That is, *land productivity* is :

$$\frac{\left(a_{42} - \dfrac{a_{12}}{a_{13}} \cdot a_{43}\right) + S\left(a_{32} - \dfrac{a_{12}}{a_{13}} \cdot a_{33}\right)}{a_{22} - \dfrac{a_{12}}{a_{13}} \cdot a_{23}}$$

or

$$\frac{\left(a_{43} - \dfrac{a_{13}}{a_{12}} \cdot a_{42}\right) + S\left(a_{33} - \dfrac{a_{13}}{a_{12}} \cdot a_{32}\right)}{a_{23} - \dfrac{a_{13}}{a_{12}} \cdot a_{22}} \, . \tag{2}$$

Productivities of labour and land with respect to Activities I and II can be similarly obtained.[1]

The Utilities of Consumption Goods

What we have said about productivities of factors applies *mutatis mutandis* to consumer utilities. In the special case where there is no element of jointness in demand, relative utilities are given simply as the ratio of the input coefficients. Suppose, for instance, that in Table 13 $a_{37} = 0$ then the utility of a unit of Output 2 is $\dfrac{1}{a_{47}}$. Similarly, if $a_{48} = 0$, the utility of a unit of Output 1 $= \dfrac{1}{a_{38}}$. The relative utilities of Outputs 1 and 2 with respect to Activities VII and VIII are then given by $\dfrac{a_{47}}{a_{38}}$. If, however, all coefficients differ from zero, the relative utilities — the consumer's substitution rates — are of the form $\dfrac{a_{47} - a_{48}}{a_{38} - a_{37}}$.

[1] For a mathematical formulation of the content of the above paragraphs, see Dorfman, *Application of Linear Programming to the Theory of the Firm*, p. 75.

Or, generally, $\dfrac{a_{ij} - a_{ik}}{a_{hk} - a_{hj}}$. We are using the consumption activities in the normalized form, so that there is only a single standardized final output (constituting a given level of satisfaction). Thus consumer utilities do not require the more complex formulae that we had to use in order to measure productivities under conditions of simultaneous joint inputs and joint outputs. Providing always that we retain the limitation that the scale of consumption does not alter consumption activities, the above simple formula expresses the relative utilities of commodities.

The above expressions become more numerous and more complicated as the number of inputs and outputs in the model is increased. It is scarcely necessary to fatigue the reader further by demonstration of this.

Comments on the Marginal Approach

The above laborious pursuit of productivities and utilities of factors and outputs serves to show the following :

(1) When we try to give empirical content to these concepts we find that they are complex, particularly the concept of productivity where jointness enters (in general) into both the input (denominator) and the output (numerator) of the ratio to which we are referring.

(2) There are as many productivities of labour as there are sets of activities — and similarly for every other input.[1] On the consumption side there are as many utilities of grain as there are sets of consumption activities — and similarly for every other output. The fact that these entities vary according to the sets of activities which are used may be regarded as the reason why economists have

---

[1] This is so even though we are assuming throughout that the multiplicity of outputs can be reduced to uniformity, i.e. we assume given relative values of consumer goods. We then express the productivities and the utilities in terms of any (arbitrarily selected) *numéraire*.

felt it necessary to stress that they are talking of *marginal* productivities and *marginal* utilities. If data changes shift the equilibrium position substantially, different activities are likely to be used, which means that the values of productivities and utilities alter.[1]

[1] An elegant formulation of substitution rates in activity tables will be found in Koopmans' article 'Maximization and Substitution in Linear Models of Production', published in *Input-Output Relations* (Netherlands Economic Institute).

CHAPTER V

THE DUAL: QUANTITIES AND PRICES

Optimal Allocation viewed as a Process of Equalizing Values

WE have been at some pains to establish from first principles the formulae (in terms of technical coefficients) which represent productivities and utilities of factors and products or, what comes to the same thing, the substitution rates between all pairs of inputs and outputs. Let us for a moment forget that we have worked out these measures of productivities and utilities, and return to the main thread of our exposition of equilibrium theory as we left it at the end of Chapter III. In that chapter we viewed the problem as one of finding the optimum quantities of resources of all kinds to be allocated to activities of all kinds. Our solution was tabulated finally in what we called the allocation matrix of Table 15, where all the x's have been determined. No reference was made anywhere to either values or prices in this analysis; and, once we know which activities are used in the equilibrium, in a way no such reference is necessary. There are no 'prices' in the sense of market prices, since we are dealing with a Crusoe economy; and since we have determined exactly how Crusoe uses his scarce resources in different production processes, and exactly what quantities of each kind of product he consumes, we know perhaps all that it is important to know.

However, there exists an alternative way of viewing the

problem. Up to now we have viewed Crusoe as allocating his resources between activities in such a way that the total amount of final consumer goods, each weighted by its respective utility, is maximized. Instead, we could view him as arranging things in such a way that, for any activity he undertakes, the *value* of what he puts in is just equal to the value of what he gets out. Even although goods have no market values in a one-man economy, they do have 'values' deriving from their (subjective) utility to Crusoe and in the case of prime resources from their potentialities for producing outputs which yield utility. If Crusoe is to maximize his utility, he will never undertake an activity in which the value of what he puts in exceeds the value of what he gets out. Furthermore, since we postulate constant returns in every activity, it can never pay him to stop in a situation where some activity shows an excess of value of output over value of input — he would shift more resources into it until the excess vanished. In other words, for any activity which is used the value of input must just equal the value of output, so that we may say that the used activities must show zero profits. Activities not used must show negative profit.

This way of looking at the equilibrium conditions leads us to a set of relationships running down the columns instead of along the rows. Thus denote the value of each of the two factors by y_1 and y_2; and that of each of the products by y_3 and y_4. Take account, moreover, of the familiar point that *in equilibrium* the value of any one commodity must be the same in all uses, or the utilization pattern would be altered. Then for the same case as we have already solved in Chapter III we can write out a matrix which we may call the value matrix for equilibrium as in Table 19.

Viewing the process of maximizing utility as one of making all used activities show zero profit, we then say that,

ACTIVITIES

	II	III	VII	VIII
Input 1	$-a_{12}y_1$	$-a_{13}y_1$	o	o
Input 2	$-a_{22}y_2$	$-a_{23}y_2$	o	o
Output 1	$a_{32}y_3$	$a_{33}y_3$	$-a_{37}y_3$	$-a_{38}y_3$
Output 2	$a_{42}y_4$	$a_{43}y_4$	$-a_{47}y_4$	$-a_{48}y_4$
Utility index	o	o	1	1

TABLE 19

if II, III, VII, and VIII are the used activities, we must have the four equations : [1]

$$a_{12}\,y_1 + a_{22}\,y_2 = a_{32}\,y_3 + a_{42}\,y_4 \qquad . \qquad . \qquad (1)$$

$$a_{13}\,y_1 + a_{23}\,y_2 = a_{33}\,y_3 + a_{43}\,y_4 \qquad . \qquad . \qquad (2)$$

$$a_{37}\,y_3 + a_{47}\,y_4 = 1 \qquad . \qquad . \qquad . \qquad (3)$$

$$a_{38}\,y_3 + a_{48}\,y_4 = 1 \qquad . \qquad . \qquad . \qquad (4)$$

The utility index 1 stands for any given level of satisfaction. We equate the left-hand side of equations (3) and (4), thereby replacing them by a single equation.

The solution of the three equations is then :

$$\frac{y_3}{y_4} = \left(\frac{a_{47}-a_{48}}{a_{38}-a_{37}}\right) \qquad . \qquad . \qquad . \qquad . \qquad . \qquad (5)$$

$$\frac{y_2}{y_4} = \frac{\left(a_{43}-\dfrac{a_{13}}{a_{12}}\cdot a_{42}\right)+\left(\dfrac{a_{47}-a_{48}}{a_{38}-a_{37}}\right)\left(a_{33}-\dfrac{a_{13}}{a_{12}}\cdot a_{32}\right)}{a_{23}-\dfrac{a_{13}}{a_{12}}\cdot a_{22}} \qquad . \qquad (6)$$

$$\frac{y_1}{y_4} = \frac{\left(a_{43}-\dfrac{a_{23}}{a_{22}}\cdot a_{42}\right)+\left(\dfrac{a_{47}-a_{48}}{a_{38}-a_{37}}\right)\left(a_{33}-\dfrac{a_{23}}{a_{22}}\cdot a_{32}\right)}{a_{13}-\dfrac{a_{23}}{a_{22}}\cdot a_{12}} \qquad . \qquad (7)$$

We express each value in terms of the value of the second output which is used as *numéraire*.

[1] For each of the unused activities, we must have *in*equalities showing value of input exceeding or equalling value of output.

The 'Dual Solution' and the Economic Concepts of Productivity and Utility

Now the first result above,

$$\frac{y_3}{y_4} = \frac{a_{47} - a_{48}}{a_{38} - a_{37}},$$

is, of course, as was stated in Chapter IV the utility to the consumer of a unit of Output 1 in terms of Output 2. It is what we denoted by S in equations (1) and (2) (pp. 48-50). That is, our solution tells us that in the equilibrium situation the imputed value (or 'internal price') of Output 2 in terms of Output 1 must be equal to the ratio of their utilities.

Further, it is seen that the solution just reached for $\frac{y_2}{y_4}$ is identical with the measure which we derived (equation 2, p. 50) from first principles for the marginal productivity of the second input, in terms of the second output. Similarly, the solution for $\frac{y_1}{y_4}$ is identical with our measure for the marginal product of the first input, in terms of the second output (equation 1, p. 49). That is, our solution tells us that in equilibrium the values imputed to factors are equal to their productivities.

It may well be felt that a proposition so familiar to economists as that imputed values are proportionate to productivities (or utilities) does not warrant the writing of several pages of elementary algebra. Perhaps not. But if we take that position it means that we are satisfied that we understand what is meant by 'marginal productivity' in complex economies and do not require any aid in finding the link between it and actual empirical activities. Probably quite a few students do not attain this understanding, but rather accept (after reiterated instructions) that marginal productivity of a factor is that which it can earn, and that which a factor can earn is its marginal productivity.

However this may be, there is another reason why we have gone back to fundamentals to establish in terms of our present activity approach the internal or imputed values of commodities in equilibrium. It is this. One of the most perplexing things to the non-mathematical economist trying to understand activity analysis is the Dual. The uninitiated reader may get the impression that, for inscrutable mathematical reasons, the constrained matrix which yields the vector of intensities [1] at which each activity will be carried on, will at the same time yield a Dual solution — another vector.[2] This vector, he is told, is (if the model is regarded as an analogue to an economy) a set of prices. The present author has found this mode of presentation frustrating. The mathematicians seem to have pulled a very large rabbit very suddenly out of a hat. Perhaps the average student making himself acquainted with the activity approach to equilibrium analysis will not get this impression that he is being introduced to the prices of the system as though they were primarily a mathematical property of constrained matrices. But the present writer has preferred to go right back to elementary economic principles and work laboriously through to the dual prices, instead of accepting them out of the hat. Once one has done this, one feels quite prepared to recognize the Dual — indeed one rather likes it. The whole thing may be compared to a woven cloth : we can study its substance by following the woof across the cloth (the row equations of our analysis of allocation above) or we can study it down the warp (the column equations of our analysis of internal values). But it is one and the same piece of cloth whichever way we analyse it — take away

---

[1] x's in our notation.
[2] See, for instance, *Activity Analysis of Production and Allocation* (Ed. T. C. Koopmans), p. 65. Dorfman in *Application of Linear Programming to the Theory of the Firm* (chap. ii, paras. 6 and 7) does, on the other hand, give a non-mathematical explanation in this connection.

either the woof or the warp, and the cloth is no more. Take away either the Quantity aspect or the Value aspect, and our economic problem is no more.

Determination of Activities to be Used

As has been pointed out above, we have nowhere in our analysis given any general prescription for finding the answer to the crucial question: which of the efficient activities will be used at all? We have worked through some very simple examples by exhaustive trial and error. In the later analysis we have supposed that we know which activities it is optimal to use, and proceeded to find the optimal quantities of resources to allocate to each, and the equilibrium values of the factors and products. By this procedure we have evaded a substantial point. We have said that the identification of those activities which it is optimal to use has to be effected by what amounts to a method of successive approximation. But the mathematicians have so systematized the process as to make it quite feasible (with the aid of computing machines) even for large matrices.

The procedure which has been generally adopted is known by the name of the Simplex method. Under this method one starts by selecting any set of activities, containing the right [1] number of activities, and pretending that this set is the equilibrium set. Accordingly, one values all the goods at such values as would make the profit on each activity in the set zero (as would be true in equilibrium). Using the values determined in this way, one then calculates the profits on every activity outside the chosen set. For some activities the profit thus computed will, in general, be negative; for others it will, in general,

---

[1] The number of activities included in the set must be equal to the number of goods (inputs plus outputs) in the system.

be positive. Whichever activity shows the largest positive profit is then to be taken into the set of used activities, in place of some activity initially included. The determination of the activity to be thrown out is automatic, since the introduction of the new activity must reduce the level of some other activity, and as no activity can be reduced to less than zero level, that activity which declines to zero most quickly as the level of the new activity is increased, must be the one to go out. The new set of activities thus formed is necessarily better than the initial set. The process is repeated, giving us solutions which are successively nearer and nearer to the optimum, until no activity outside the set shows a positive profit. When this is true, we have reached the equilibrium set of activities, that is, we have identified those activities which are used in equilibrium.[1]

[1] The clearest non-mathematical exposition of the Simplex method known to the writer is contained in an unpublished paper by Mrs. Land of the London School of Economics. For mathematical expositions, see the references in Chapter II (footnote to p. 35).

CHAPTER VI

PRODUCTION FUNCTIONS, PREFERENCE FUNCTIONS, AND THE STRUCTURE OF TECHNOLOGIES

Conditions for Variable Rates of Substitution in Production and Consumption

THE representation of the technologies of production and consumption in the form of the columns of the activity matrix carries with it the implication that, *technically*, an activity can be carried on at any level. This means first, that resources are infinitely divisible, implying that the resources allocated to any activity may be varied continuously rather than discontinuously; and that activities are additive, implying that the outputs and inputs in any activity (production or consumption) are constant irrespective of the 'intensity' or scale upon which it, or any other activity, is undertaken. As economists we are inclined to describe this situation as one of 'constant returns to scale' in production and consumption. The assumption of such conditions may appear to be a grave defect, threatening the acceptability of the whole system. Some will probably feel disposed to grant, anyhow for the sake of argument, 'constant returns' in production, but few will feel easy about 'constant returns' in consumption. Common sense tells us that wants are satiable and that utility diminishes with increased consumption.

After considerable thought on this charge, which runs very deep, the writer has come to the conclusion that the best method of defence is attack. As we understand it, the position accepted by the majority of economists is that production conditions are such that factors of production employed in the production of a given output are, in general, only substitutable for each other at increasing rates, and that outputs arising from a given input are similarly only substitutable for each other at decreasing rates; and finally that tastes are such that consumer goods can be substituted for each other only at increasing rates (satisfaction being here held at a constant level).

In terms of geometry, isoquants (drawn in Cartesian co-ordinates measuring one factor along each axis) are convex to the origin: production possibility curves (drawn in Cartesian co-ordinates measuring one output along each axis) are concave to the origin; and indifference curves (drawn in Cartesian co-ordinates measuring one consumer good along each axis) are convex to the origin. It also seems to be widely held that on the production side a homogeneous function (and still more a linear homogeneous one) is something of a special case; and on the consumption side a homogeneous function is highly improbable, since it implies unit income-elasticity in respect of all goods, while a linear homogeneous consumption function is definitely unacceptable, since it conflicts with the satiability of wants. In terms of geometry, successive isoquants are not, in general, of the same shape; successive production opportunity curves are not, in general, of the same shape; and successive indifference curves are very unlikely to be of the same shape. Finally the 'distance between' successive curves is, in each case, likely to vary.

Consider, for instance, the following figures:

	ACTIVITIES		
	I	II	III
Input 1	− 10	− 9	− 8
Input 2	− 1	− 3	− 6
Output	1	1	1

These might depict a sector of the commonly used isoquant (approximated by linear segments). All three activities would be efficient activities.

If we consider the variations in the implied amounts of factors used in that isoquant, we see that they are as follows:

SUBSTITUTION BETWEEN ACTIVITIES:

	I and II	II and III
Input 1	-1	-1
Input 2	$+2$	$+3$
Output	0	0

If the entire list of relevant variables has been covered (i.e. only two kinds of factors and one kind of good), is the rate of substitution between Input 1 and Input 2 likely in fact to change? If two units of the latter replaced one of the former for a small substitution, what, in the technology itself, prevents further substitution at the same rate?

This point has its application to systems containing many inputs and many outputs: uncompensated changes in the marginal variations of one input (or output) are unexplained. For instance, with three inputs, the matrix

	ACTIVITIES				VARIATIONS IN INPUTS AND OUTPUTS	
Input 1	-10	-9	-8	would imply	-1	-1
Input 2	-1	-3	-6		$+2$	$+3$
Input 3	-5	-5	-5		0	0
Output	1	1	1		0	0

for which we have no obvious explanation. On the other hand, it would be quite understandable to have a matrix

	ACTIVITIES				VARIATIONS IN INPUTS AND OUTPUTS	
Input 1	-10	-9	-8	implying	-1	-1
Input 2	-1	-3	-6		$+2$	$+3$
Input 3	-5	-5	-4		0	-1
Output	1	1	1		0	0

since here the greater addition of Input 2 in the last column is offset by a shrinkage in Input 3. This would, of course, not produce a convex isoquant 'other things equal'; the isoquant in the Input 1/Input 2 space would be convex, other things unequal.

Exactly the same point arises in connection with the production possibility curve: varying rates of substitution arising in the technology itself do not seem very plausible.

It does not seem necessary to depict varying rates of substitution as a characteristic of technology itself. This does not mean that the writer suggests robbing economics of its 'increasing marginal costs' and its 'diminishing marginal utility'. What is suggested is that these features are not best regarded as features of the *technologies* of production (or consumption) but rather as arising from the existence of limitational elements in the system. In our formulation, the body of the matrix, representing pure technology, need not in itself give rise to any form of increasing costs or substitution rates. It says that if a given increase in the use of an activity is made, then there will be a strictly proportionate increase in all inputs and outputs.

To account for changing substitution rates in production and/or consumption we have to take into account not the body of the matrix alone, but also its boundary conditions, which represent the limitational factors. It is through these that we bring back variable rates of substitution in production and consumption into the economic system in our formulation; and again it is these which impart to the system so-called diminishing returns to scale of production. This may be illustrated as follows. Consider first the isoquant. This depicts varying factor bundles which produce 'a given quantity of output'. On our interpretation, if the isoquant is convex (if factor substitution rates are not constant) and if output is really constant for each factor combination, then there is some hidden third factor which is not. Thus if we add a third limitational factor — it might be storage space available in the premises, or the manager's time, or some much less easily identifiable element — we should get a matrix of the following type :

ACTIVITIES

	I	II	III	IV
Input 1	− 10	− 9	− 8	− 8
Input 2	− 1	− 3	− 5	− 6
The Third Factor	− 1	− 3	− 5	− 2
Output	1	1	1	1

TABLE 20

Now if we suppose that there is a rigidly fixed amount of the third factor, say 4 units, and then ask how the substitution rate between the two inputs behaves as Input 2 is substituted for Input 1 (i.e. as we shift from Activity I in the direction of Activity IV), we should arrive at the desired conclusion : the rate rises against Input 2. This is because Activity III (which would have kept the substitution rate constant) is ruled out by insufficiency of the third factor.[1]

A formally quite similar manipulation may be applied to preference functions in order to obtain increasing rates of substitution between consumer goods. If the figures

$$
\begin{array}{ccc}
-10 & -9 & -8 \\
-1 & -3 & -6 \\
1 & 1 & 1
\end{array}
$$

are put forward as a section of an 'indifference curve', indicating three equally desired combinations of two consumption goods, then we may explain why the substitution rate changes from 1 to 2, to 1 to 3, by assuming the influence of a third good, available in fixed quantity.

---

[1] An alternative interpretation would be to assume, instead of the hidden third factor, a dual output of varying composition, but always having a given total value or utility. An example of such a case is given by Morton in *Economica*, November 1951, 'Notes on Linear Programming', section 3.

Just as in the case of the isoquant, there may be too little of this good to permit of continued substitution of the second good for the first at fixed rates.

Finally, consider a production opportunity function of the type:

| Output 1 | 36 | 32 | 28 |
| Output 2 | 8 | 16 | 17 |

It is usually said that these combinations are produced from 'given resources'. If we interpret this to mean a given quantity of a single factor, we should not be able to explain the diminishing returns in the above figures. If we suppose that there are two factors, each available (but not necessarily *used*) in fixed total amounts, then we can arrive at the 'diminishing returns' for the outputs. Thus suppose that the following production activities produce the two outputs (we take a very simple example, without joint outputs):

Input 1	−10	−5
Input 2	−2	−8
Output 1	4	0
Output 2	0	4

Suppose, further, that the amount of the primary resources available are 100 of Input 1 and 48 of Input 2. Then the maximum outputs for which there would be enough of Input 1, are 40 of Output 1 *or* 80 of Output 2, or any linear combination of these. Similarly, the maximum amounts of outputs for which there would be enough of Input 2 are 96 of Output 1 or 24 of Output 2, or any linear combination of these. Since *both* factors must be sufficient, the maximum amount of Output 1 is 40, that of Output 2 is 24. If 40 of Output 1 is produced (and none of Output 2) some of Input 2 is unused; if 24 of Output 2 is produced (and none of Output 1) some of Input 1 is unused. If 32 of Output 1 and 16 of Output 2 is produced, the total available amounts of both factors are exactly used up. As the amount of Output 1 is varied from 40 to 32 (with that of Output 2 varying from 0 to 16) Input 1 is the only effectively scarce factor, and the substitution rate between the outputs is governed by the ratio of their coefficients of Input 1. That is, since half as much of this Input is used per unit Output 2 as is used per unit Output 1, the substitution rate between the two outputs is, while Input 1 is the only scarce factor, held constant at 2 : 1. As the amount of Output 1 is varied from 32 to 0 (with that of Output 2 varying from 16 to 24) Input 2 is the only scarce factor. The substitution rate between the outputs is, over this range of variation, held constant at the ratio of the Input 2 coefficients, namely 1 : 4.[1]

Incorporation of Latent Variables

It will be understood that in all the cases discussed here we have to suppose that there are as many 'suppressed variables' as there are different substitution rates in excess of that number accounted for by the explicit variables. Thus with the production opportunity curve two factors will produce one kink in the boundary (two substitution rates). Three factors will produce two kinks, and so forth. Similarly with the indifference curve. The inclusion of all these extra variables in all our tables would be tedious and should be unnecessary once the principle is established. We therefore show in full below the effect upon the table of introducing into the consumption function one shadow good. In all subsequent tables we leave the reader to supply his own shadow limitational commodities to secure varying returns to scale.

Thus, suppose that the utility derived from any consumer activity depends both upon identifiable consumer goods and services, and also upon one other unknown

[1] Alternatively, a third output may be introduced in such a way as to yield convexity in the Output 1/Output 2 space.

good, of which there is a limited amount. The activity matrix which we are writing thus:

	ACTIVITIES			RESOURCES
	PRODUCTION		CONSUMPTION	
	I	II	III	
f_1	$-a_{11}$	$-a_{12}$	0	$\geqslant -b_1$
f_2	$-a_{21}$	$-a_{22}$	0	$\geqslant -b_2$
g_1	a_{31}	a_{32}	$-a_{33}$	$\geqslant 0$
g_2	a_{41}	a_{42}	$-a_{43}$	$\geqslant 0$
	0	0	c_1	Max.

TABLE 21

then becomes:

	ACTIVITIES					RESOURCES
	PRODUCTION		CONSUMPTION			
	I	II	III	IV	V	
f_1	$-a_{11}$	$-a_{12}$	0	0	0	$\geqslant -b_1$
f_2	$-a_{21}$	$-a_{22}$	0	0	0	$\geqslant -b_2$
g_1	a_{31}	a_{32}	$-a_{33}$	$-a_{33}$	$-a_{33}$	$\geqslant 0$
g_2	a_{41}	a_{42}	$-a_{43}$	$-a_{43}$	$-a_{43}$	$\geqslant 0$
γ (Shadow Good)	0	0	$-b_5$	$-\dfrac{b_5}{n}$	$-\dfrac{b_5}{n.m}$	$\geqslant -b_5$
	0	0	c_1	c_2	c_3	Max.

where $1 < n$, m and $\dfrac{c_1}{n} < c_2 < c_1$; $\dfrac{c_2}{m} < c_3 < c_2$.

TABLE 22

Here the unknown element which fails to increase (and hence causes utility to fail to increase in proportion) as the amounts consumed of the two produced consumer goods increase, is γ. If consumption of the two goods is at level one, utility is c_1; if it is raised above one, the amount of the unknown good combined with the amounts a_{33} and a_{43} of the two commodities falls, so that utility falls; and so on progressively, as the level of consumption of the two

A.A.—F

commodities is raised. This representation can be extended to any number of different patterns of consumer good combinations by introducing an extra limited good in respect of each.

Interpretation of Latent Variables

The above paragraphs will scarcely be acceptable to all readers. We may be able to attribute a plain meaning to the suppressed variables behind the production opportunity curve (multiplicity of regular factors of production) and perhaps to those behind the isoquant (multiplicity of outputs). But what are the fixed extra consumption goods which are not produced ? Certainly their credentials should be questioned. But the right point to start questioning seems to be, not 'What is the shadow good, γ, in the matrix ?' but rather 'What causes the same consumption good bundle to yield less satisfaction as the amount consumed increases ?' This seems the right point to start questioning if we are to start at all. But our prospects of finding an answer seem poor. As economists we are more likely to get somewhere in pursuing the Third Man in production functions than in preference functions, which are scarcely susceptible to economic analysis. It would be very difficult to find any empirical basis for shadow consumer goods, or to ascribe a meaning to them.

Some people may accept our formulation as one which reproduces the relationships required by economic theory, without attempting to attach any empirical meaning to the shadow commodities which are implied in the model. Others may feel uncomfortable about working with a formal device whose economic meaning is unclear. We shall not try to interpret these shadow figures here. We shall be content if we have succeeded in showing that the necessity for introducing extra goods arises in the traditional analysis itself. The activity formulation used here is not responsible for them; it merely exposes them.

'Returns to Scale' in the Relevant Sense are variable in our Model

It may be objected that the need to create all these extra variables is merely a consequence of over-fine definitions of factors and products. There is, of course, a valid point here — with broad enough definitions one would not have to distinguish between any economic variables: it is all a matter of classification. But we reach now the last point which we have to make. If we are allowed our definitions, and with them our extra variables, then the charge against the validity of the present formulation of the economic system that it implies constant returns to scale not only in production but also in consumption, falls to the ground. For those same shadow factors and shadow goods which have to be introduced in order to justify the production functions and preference functions of traditional analysis are sufficient to eliminate from our system constant returns to scale, in the relevant sense. Our formulation does mean, as has already been said, that each technical process can be carried on at any level, and maintain its input-output relationship. But when we take into account the boundary conditions of our technological matrix we find that the fixity of the shadow consumer goods will eliminate the unsuitable characteristic that a doubling of utility can be obtained by a doubling of the activities used. Similarly, fixed factors of production may serve to prevent a doubling of production from inevitably accompanying a doubling of variable prime factors.

The homogeneity or otherwise of the production function on the one hand, and of the consumption function on the other, must depend upon what elements we include *as variables* in each respective function. Variable returns may be secured by including in the functions some sort of element which does not vary proportionately with the rest. Under our interpretation such 'fixed elements' are incorporated in the boundary conditions, and excluded from the body of the matrix which represents technologies. It is to be noted that 'scale of production' is to be measured by reference to the real goods only. We have 'diminishing returns to scale of production' if double the output uses up more than double the input of *the variable prime factors* which are scarce (a shadow factor is fixed and does not double; nor does a factor which had not been fully utilized).

Similarly, if utility were measurable we should have 'diminishing utility in consumption' if double the utility required more than double the amounts of the variable scarce consumer goods (shadow goods would not double, nor would free goods).

Whether or not the introduction (or exposure) of these twilight goods and factors is satisfactory, it seems clear that any difficulty about constant or variable returns to scale, and appropriate behaviour of substitution rates, is a difficulty attaching to accepted economic theory. If the present formulation is unacceptable on this score, we shall have to draw the inference for traditional analysis. This seems to be one of the many instances in which an obviously questionable point in the activity formulation of the economic system turns out to be a concealed questionable point in traditional analysis. It is one of the main advantages of using the activity formulation that it highlights weak points while the traditional approach often allows them to remain concealed.

The above paragraphs are directed towards the phenomenon of 'decreasing returns' rather than that of 'increasing returns'. As regards the latter, the present treatment does not differ from traditional treatment at this point: the prevalence of increasing returns in the system as a whole, which would be incompatible with equilibrium, is still precluded by assumption.[1]

---

[1] An interesting contribution to the analysis of the subject matter of this chapter will be found in Mr. John Chipman's article 'Linear Programming', *Review of Economics and Statistics*, May 1953. See also Koopmans, *Activity Analysis of Production and Allocation*, chap. iii.

CHAPTER VII

ALLOCATION OF RESOURCES IN AN
OPEN EXCHANGE ECONOMY

Introductory

IN the preceding chapters we have been at some pains to
avoid basing our analysis on market prices, but to present
it in terms of quantities and substitution rates in consumption and production. The existence of both kinds of
substitution rate — of productivities and of utilities — is
logically prior to, and entirely independent of, the existence
of 'prices' in the ordinary sense of market prices; the
substitution rates exist whether or not a market exists. If
we describe the equilibrium set of substitution rates as
'shadow prices' or 'accounting prices', that is merely
another name for equilibrium substitution rates. These
rates constitute, of course, the rates at which goods will be
exchanged on a market, that is, they *become* market prices,
if there happens to be a market. But in almost any comparative statics problem, prices are liable to change because
the forces behind them change. To analyse problems
involving a sizable sector of economic activities — such
as foreign trade, or investment — in terms of market
prices is like constructing a building on shifting sands.
The formulation of the data used in activity analysis with
its clearly distinguishable substitution rates between every
pair of activities and its sharply defined solution should
perhaps help to prevent confusion between the sets of
basic physical and psychological 'swop-rates' on the one

hand and the particular set of values which obtains in equilibrium on the other. The fact that we must not beg basic questions of substitution rates does not, however, mean that it is desirable to limit our analysis to the study of economic activity in the absence of exchange. In the present chapter we turn over to partial equilibrium analysis and consider an individual (or group) exchanging in markets where the prices (whether constant or varying with quantities exchanged) are *data* of the problem.

An Entrepreneur Buying in a Perfect Market

In Chapters II and III we considered how a farmer or manufacturer or transport undertaking would arrange production (in given demand conditions) if he had absolutely fixed quantities of prime resources. In reality entrepreneurs can vary the quantities of most resources by purchasing on the market. Consider first the simplest possible form of economy with exchange: an economy where people exchange and consume, but do not produce. *If the prices at which things are exchanged can be taken as constant*, this situation can very easily be translated into the same form as our production economy. Suppose we imagine that the farmer, instead of planning his production arrangements on his farm, is to plan purchases in a market. In effect all we do is to reduce each person's number of limitational factors to one. We may if we like call this particular individual's limited factor 'money'. The supply of money must be limited in the present problem; for we are assuming that infinite quantities can be bought at given prices, and that no production activities take place, so that there are no physical limitations in operation. Hence unless money is limited there can be no economic problem at all.

Let the price of Output 1 be p_1 and that of Output 2 be p_2. Then the matrix of expenditures on each process at unit level is:

$$a_{11}p_1 \qquad a_{12}p_1 \qquad a_{13}p_1$$
$$a_{21}p_2 \qquad a_{22}p_2 \qquad a_{23}p_2$$

TABLE 23

The producer is trying to choose that process or combination of processes which will maximize consumption subject to his money limitation.

Since he gets one unit of final output for
$$(a_{11}p_1 + a_{21}p_2) \text{ in Process I}$$
and also for
$$(a_{12}p_1 + a_{22}p_2) \text{ in Process II}$$
and also for
$$(a_{13}p_1 + a_{23}p_2) \text{ in Process III}$$
it is clear that he will employ all his money (M) on whichever process costs the least. His maximum consumption is equal to the greatest of the following:

$$\frac{M}{a_{11}p_1 + a_{21}p_2} \; ; \; \frac{M}{a_{12}p_1 + a_{22}p_2} \; ; \; \frac{M}{a_{13}p_1 + a_{23}p_2}.$$

An Entrepreneur Producing and Buying in a Perfect Market

We want now to depict the situation in which the producer is both buying on the market and producing. Imagine a producer with certain physical resources (land, plant, etc.) and a fixed amount of money capital (this might be the entrepreneur's own capital, or he might have permission to borrow up to a limited sum from the bank). The activity matrix for production and exchange may be formulated in the following way. For simplicity we show the case where there is only one type of output. We suppose further that only two kinds of physical input are used in each process. The market price of Input 1 is p_1 and that of Input 2 is p_2. Then we have a matrix of the following form : [1]

	PRODUCTION ACTIVITIES						RESOURCES
	With initial resources		With purchased resources				
	I	II	III	IV	V	VI	
Money	0	0	$-p_1$	$-p_2$	0	0	$\geqslant -M$
Input 1	$-a_{21}$	$-a_{22}$	0	0	0	0	$\geqslant -K$
Input 2	$-a_{31}$	$-a_{32}$	0	0	0	0	$\geqslant -L$
Input 3	0	0	1	0	$-a_{45}$	$-a_{46}$	$\geqslant 0$
Input 4	0	0	0	1	$-a_{55}$	$-a_{56}$	$\geqslant 0$
Output	1	1	0	0	1	1	Max.

TABLE 24

Here the producer has a fixed money capital $= M$
a fixed stock of Factor 1 = K
a fixed stock of Factor 2 = L

and Inputs 1 and 3 are identical, as are Inputs 2 and 4. But this need not necessarily be so.

This matrix can be extended to cover more complex cases. The number of outputs and inputs may be increased, and consumer activities added. No new principles enter, either in the formulation or the solution of the problem. The necessary addition to the procedure used in the analysis of a producer doing no exchange is simply the addition of the activities of purchasing factors (III and IV) at the given market prices and of producing with purchased factors (V and VI), and the inclusion of the constraint upon total purchases, represented by the entrepreneur's available cash (M).

[1] If Processes V and VI, undertaken with purchased resources, are technically identical with Processes I and II respectively, then the matrix would be reduced, as follows :

	I	II	III	IV		
Money	0	0	$-p_1$	$-p_2$	$\geqslant -M$	
Input 1	$-a_{21}$	$-a_{22}$	1	0	$\geqslant -K$	
Input 2	$-a_{31}$	$-a_{32}$	0	1	$\geqslant -L$	
Output	1	1	0	0	Max.	

The constraints will be:

$$a_{21}x_1 + a_{22}x_2 \leqslant K$$
$$a_{31}x_1 + a_{32}x_2 \leqslant L$$
$$p_1x_3 + p_2x_4 \leqslant M$$
$$x_3 - a_{45}x_5 - a_{46}x_6 \geqslant 0$$
$$x_4 - a_{55}x_5 - a_{56}x_6 \geqslant 0$$

where

p_1 is the market price of Input 3

p_2 ,, ,, ,, 4.

In this example where there are only five scarce factors the optimal solution will not require the use of more than five activities,[1] which will be determined from the five relationships.

Alternatively, if we approach the problem from the angle of productivity instead of allocation, we have the six inequalities:

$$-a_{21}y_2 - a_{31}y_3 + y_6 \leqslant 0$$
$$-a_{22}y_2 - a_{32}y_3 + y_6 \leqslant 0$$
$$-p_1y_1 + y_3 \leqslant 0$$
$$-p_2y_1 + y_4 \leqslant 0$$
$$-a_{45}y_4 - a_{55}y_5 + y_6 \leqslant 0$$
$$-a_{46}y_4 - a_{56}y_5 + y_6 \leqslant 0.$$

Of these only five will, in general, be equalities in the optimum position. The values for the optimal substitution ratios (the relative prices of the goods)

$$\frac{y_5}{y_2} \quad \frac{y_4}{y_2} \quad \frac{y_3}{y_2} \quad \frac{y_1}{y_2}$$

are obtained by the solution of the five equations which determine the five y's. These optimum substitution rates give the prices at which inputs will exchange in the market.

An Entrepreneur Dealing in Imperfect Markets

In reality the prices at which a person can exchange things — whether inputs or outputs — are often not

[1] See Chapter X.

constant. The generalization of our analysis to enable us to comprise within it exchange at varying prices is slightly more complex than the generalization from production without exchange to production with exchange at constant prices.

First, it is obvious that once the simple assumption of constant prices is abandoned we have to put in its place some *data* specifying the way in which prices vary. There is an infinity of ways in which prices could vary; to render our problem determinate we must be given a specific rule of variation. Thus, for instance, economists working with supply and demand functions, who wish to consider prices which vary with quantity consumed, often postulate a linear function relating price and quantity. In what follows we postulate certain step functions.

Given the function relating quantities exchanged with price paid per unit exchanged, we may depict this by showing a separate exchange activity for each price. The quantity which can be exchanged at any given price becomes a boundary condition in the matrix formulation. Thus in Table 25 we depict an economy in which the entrepreneur buys his factors of production in imperfect markets. There are available only L_1 units of labour at price p_1; a further L_2 units are available at price p_2. An unlimited quantity is available at the highest price p_3. Similarly, the second factor of production is only available in limited quantity (K_1) at price p_4; a further limited quantity (K_2) at price p_5; and an unlimited quantity at the highest price p_6. Assuming that the entrepreneur's total money supply is limited, and that we know the technical production processes relating inputs of factors with output of the final good (whether money or physical), the data are then sufficient for determining the optimal solution. In Table 25 we show just two technical processes (Activities VII and VIII) and one final product.

Some people may interpret this formulation of exchange conditions under varying prices as an approximation to the real situation where prices vary continuously with quantity sold, instead of discontinuously. Others may be inclined to think that the formulation in which prices vary continuously is an approximation to the real situation in which prices vary discontinuously from seller to seller,

	ACTIVITIES								RESOURC
	I	II	III	IV	V	VI	VII	VIII	
Labour available in Market 1	-1	o	o	o	o	o	o	o	$\geqslant -L_1$
Labour available in Market 2	o	-1	o	o	o	o	o	o	$\geqslant -L_2$
Machinery available in Market 1	o	o	o	-1	o	o	o	o	$\geqslant -K_1$
Machinery available in Market 2	o	o	o	o	-1	o	o	o	$\geqslant -K_2$
Money	$-p_1$	$-p_2$	$-p_3$	$-p_4$	$-p_5$	$-p_6$	o	o	
Labour	1	1	1	o	o	o	$-a_{11}$	$-a_{12}$	$\geqslant$ o
Machinery	o	o	o	1	1	1	$-a_{21}$	$-a_{22}$	$\geqslant$ o
Output	o	o	o	o	o	o	1	1	Max.

TABLE 25

area to area, etc. It does not very much matter if we disagree what 'the real situation' is (it will, of course, vary widely from problem to problem), so long as we agree that either approach may be used as an approximation to the other.

We may depict imperfect markets for products in a similar way. Here again we must know the function relating quantity sold with price fetched. Suppose that an entrepreneur with given money capital is producing two kinds of output for sale. Let the quantity of the first output which can be sold at the highest price, p_1, be N_1; that which can be sold at the second highest price, p_2, be N_2; and suppose that at the lowest price p_3 the producer can sell any quantity. Similarly, for the second output the quantity S_1 can be sold at p_4; S_2 can be sold at p_5; and any further quantity at p_6. We should then formulate the data as in Table 26 (no technical details of inputs are shown here; the table may be interpreted either as giving only a shorthand representation of the production activities, or else as a representation of the activities of a middleman who buys the products with his money capital and re-sells them at a profit).

	ACTIVITIES								RESOURCES
	I	II	III	IV	V	VI	VII	VIII	
oney	$-a_{11}$	$-a_{12}$	o	o	o	o	o	o	$\geqslant -M$
tput 1	a_{21}	a_{22}	-1	-1	-1	o	o	o	$\geqslant$ o
tput 2	a_{31}	a_{32}	o	o	o	-1	-1	-1	$\geqslant$ o
tput 1 sold in Market 1	o	o	-1	o	o	o	o	o	$\geqslant -N_1$
tput 1 sold in Market 2	o	o	o	-1	o	o	o	o	$\geqslant -N_2$
tput 2 sold in Market 1	o	o	o	o	o	-1	o	o	$\geqslant -S_1$
tput 2 sold in Market 2	o	o	o	o	o	o	-1	o	$\geqslant -S_2$
ceipts	o	o	p_1	p_2	p_3	p_4	p_5	p_6	Max.

TABLE 26

Conclusion

Although we have generalized our treatment of exchange to allow of both exchange and production being found in the economy, to allow of variable consumption patterns, and to allow of imperfect markets, yet the treatment is still 'partial'. It subsumes equilibrium market prices established somehow in the economy at large, by the aid of which it establishes equilibrium in that particular part of it which is examined — the equilibrium quantities bought, produced, and consumed by a particular individual.

In other words, we have put into the activity formulation on the one hand the general theory of equilibrium quantities and internal 'prices' in a Crusoe economy; and on the other hand the partial equilibrium theory of an individual buying and selling in a 'given' market. What we have not presented in activity terms is the theory of exchange itself. The fact that this will not be found in this book is an indication of the frontiers of useful application of the technique we are using, at least as far as the present writer is able to discern them (others may already have seen further and pushed beyond these frontiers). Although, as we have seen, it is quite simple to incorporate buying and selling from outside the system (partial equilibrium analysis) it is much less easy to incorporate buying and selling within the system. It is not impossible to do this; but so far as the present writer is acquainted with them, the resulting tabulations are so clumsy as to be of little aid to clear thinking. Perhaps this problem of neat representation of exchange within the economy will soon be solved. Perhaps, on the contrary, there lies at the bottom of the difficulty a basic deficiency in the theory of market behaviour which in our rigid formulation it becomes impossible to conceal?

Part 2

PURE THEORY OF TAXATION AND SPECIALIZATION: PROBLEMS IN NON-OPTIMAL ALLOCATION OF RESOURCES

CHAPTER VIII

THE PURE THEORY OF TAXATION

Direct and Indirect Taxes

ASSUME that some authority (such as the government) imposes upon an economy a tax which is to have a given yield in real terms, i.e. to provide a given set of physical goods. Given the amount of these physical goods which the government is going to take away through taxation, which method of raising funds for obtaining these resources is best? The familiar answer to this is that 'direct' taxation is best, since indirect taxation leads to shifts away from the optimal allocation in production and consumption. Ricardo put the point quite clearly.

'If a tax were laid on home manufacture', he wrote, there would be 'an increased price caused by the difficulty of production, which is incurred because the easiest means of production are taken away from us by being fettered with a tax.' [1] And again, 'taxes on the transference of property . . . prevent the national capital from being distributed in the way most beneficial to the community. For the general prosperity there cannot be too much facility given to the conveyance and exchange of all kinds of property.' [2] Taxes imposed on the production or consumption of particular goods or groups of goods, or upon transference — whether legal (i.e. exchanging ownership) or physical (i.e. re-allocating resources) — generally involve waste. For the existence of such taxes means, in

[1] *Principles of Political Economy and Taxation*, Chapter VIII.
[2] *Ibid.*

general, that there is not only the subtraction of the given amount of real resources from the economy by the state; but, in addition, a shift of production and/or consumption activities over and above any shift that might be required for the optimal arrangement after the payment of a given real levy to the government.

While it is common knowledge that inefficiency is introduced by 'indirect' taxation, it is not always clearly understood what constitutes the difference between indirect and direct taxes. Thus, Little and Friedman [1] have shown that income tax need not be more efficient than commodity taxes. Little has pointed out that it is poll tax rather then income tax which qualifies for the property ascribed to a direct tax. He concludes that taxes should be levied upon goods with 'zero elasticity of supply', i.e. available in given quantity. The formulation used in the present text dissolves by its very rigidity the confusions arising about direct and indirect taxes.

The Representation of Taxes in Kind

Thus let us consider an economy with a single consumer, with two factors of production, two types of output and variable production and consumption activities — we show just two of each. This economy is depicted in Table 27.

This Table is just the same as those previously used. In the absence of outside interference the individual's objective of maximizing his utility leads to the determination of the optimal scales upon which to carry on each activity (the x vector) and this solution implies a given set of factor and output values (the y vector).

If the government levies a tax in kind upon the

[1] I. M. D. Little, 'Direct *versus* Indirect Taxes', *Economic Journal*, September 1951. M. Friedman, 'The "Welfare" Effects of an Income Tax and an Excise Tax', *Journal of Political Economy*, February 1952. See also the article by Phipps and Friedman in the same journal of August 1952, 'Friedman's "Welfare" Effects'.

economy, this is shown in our formulation by additional
constraints upon the quantities of resources shown on the

	ACTIVITIES				RESOURCES
	I	II	III	IV	
Intensities	x_1	x_2	x_3	x_4	
Equilibrium Values :					
y_1 Labour	$-a_{11}$	$-a_{12}$	0	0	$\geqslant -b_1$
y_2 Land	$-a_{21}$	$-a_{22}$	0	0	$\geqslant -b_2$
y_3 Meat	a_{31}	a_{32}	$-a_{33}$	$-a_{34}$	$\geqslant 0$
y_4 Grain	a_{41}	a_{42}	$-a_{43}$	$-a_{44}$	$\geqslant 0$
	0	0	c_3	c_4	Max.

TABLE 27

right hand of the body of the matrix, that is, upon the *b*
vector. If, for instance, the government is to have a
certain quantity of meat, this means that instead of the
zero in the third row of the column of entries under
'Resources' we should have some quantity, say, b'_3, the
value of which would be the amount of the levy. Similarly,
if the government were to levy soccage of so many labour
days, the labour available to the private economy would be
less than before — say, b'_1 instead of b_1. Thus, in general,
we can formulate the data of the economy inclusive of
taxes in kind as follows :

ACTIVITIES				RESOURCES
I	II	III	IV	
$-a_{11}$	$-a_{12}$	0	0	$\geqslant -b'_1$
$-a_{21}$	$-a_{22}$	0	0	$\geqslant -b'_2$
a_{31}	a_{32}	$-a_{33}$	$-a_{34}$	$\geqslant b'_3$
a_{41}	a_{42}	$-a_{43}$	$-a_{44}$	$\geqslant b'_4$
0	0	c_3	c_4	Max.

TABLE 28

In consequence of the new constraints upon the
system — the necessity to surrender goods and perhaps

factors of production to the government — the optimum allocation of resources will, in general, be different from what it was before the tax. There will be a new set of x's and a new set of y's for the optimal utilization of the resources remaining to the private consumer. The new pattern of allocation and relative values will, in general, be unique. That is, given that the consumer has to surrender certain goods to the government, there is, in general, only *one* best way of arranging his resources to meet his desires and his tax. Any method of levying the given tax burden which distorts the arrangement away from this particular pattern is wasteful.

The Four Types of Taxation

Now it may be seen that in terms of the matrix there are four ways of levying taxation :

(1) Direct levy in kind (constraint upon the b vector).

(2) A levy upon the consumer's final utilities. (Constraint upon the c vector.) Such a tax is not found in reality.

(3) Taxes on goods. Instances of such taxes are *ad valorem* and specific taxes attaching to particular goods.

(4) Taxes on activities. These include licences, stamp duty, entertainment taxes.

Methods (3) and (4) constitute constraints upon the y vector, the x vector, or both.

Of these four ways the first is, as we have said, efficient. That is, it allows the consumer to retain the highest possible utility after surrendering the bill of goods fixed by the government. Method (2) is not used. Taxes affecting prices of goods and those affecting scale of activities are dual to each other in the sense that every constraint upon the y vector, such as a system of *ad valorem* excise duties, implies a certain alteration in the x vector, so that the same solution may be reached either by constraints upon prices or by corresponding constraints upon activities. Although by special coincidence Methods (3) and (4) might be innocuous — the government might 'hit-off' just that set of prices and allocations which would result from a levy in kind — they are, in general, wasteful. For they mean that the individual is adapting his production arrangements not to his needs for himself and the tax, but to an arbitrary price pattern or allocation pattern. This is the rationale of point rationing of consumers introduced during the war. The government wished to take away from the public certain scarce basic resources — principally shipping space. The most efficient way of making this levy was to limit the shipping allocated to food imports, and allow the consumer to utilize his allocation as he liked. The issue of point rationing books effected this.

Thus, taxation involves the two analytically distinct features : the removal of goods from the economy and the imposition of constraints upon the system. Taking the first as given, we may analyse the second in isolation by setting up an example where the amount of revenue to be raised is zero and the government imposes the constraints commonly used for raising positive (or sometimes negative) amounts of revenue, i.e. we may suppose that a price constraint is imposed which is neither prohibitive nor accompanied by the collecting of revenue. The government simply decrees that the economy must conserve a substitution rate with respect to certain pairs of activities which differs from the substitution rate operating with respect to another pair of used activities. To fix ideas, suppose that the decree says that the substitution rate operating in production activities must differ from that operating in consumption activities. Price constraints of this sort amount to an order forbidding optimal allocation of resources. The producer is ordered so to allocate his resources that substitution rates vary for different used activities. Such allocation is not optimal. This is what is meant when it is said that 'price discrimination' or 'price distortion' involves economic loss. The principle at work is the same whether the revenue to be raised is positive, zero, or negative.

The whole of the above reasoning applies, *mutatis mutandis*, to government subsidies. If given real resources are to be spent in subsidization, this would be best done in kind rather than indirectly through constraining prices and allocation. The representation of subsidies is already covered in our Table 28, for we may allow b'_3 and b'_4 to be negative quantities — amounts given to the economy by the government. Similarly, the amounts of available factors (b'_1 and b'_2) may be either less than or greater than the amounts (b_1 and b_2 in Table 25) owned by the private consumer. If they are greater, this represents free government provision of factors.

Some Geometrical Illustrations of Taxation Principles

The above formulation of the effect of differing systems of collecting a given tax gives substantially the same results as the various geometrical constructions which have been employed in this field. Fig. 3a below reproduces a diagram long used in theoretical discussion of this point.[1] If AT represents money income of the individual, AS the commodity he is buying, and the curves i_0, i_1, i_2 . . . his indifference curves related to the origin A; then if market price is constant and measured by the slope TR', the optimum point for him is at P where TR' produced is tangent to an indifference curve. If the government

[1] See M. F. W. Joseph, 'The Excess Burden of Indirect Taxation', *Review of Economic Studies*, June 1939. M. Friedman, *op. cit.*, *Journal of Political Economy*, February 1952, and I. M. D. Little, *op. cit.*, *Economic Journal*, September 1951.

requires to take an amount of money TT′ from the individual, they can either take it in the form of direct levy, leaving price uninfluenced, which will give a new equilibrium at Q; alternatively, they can impose a tax on the buying price of the commodity of such a magnitude that those buying it are willing to give out for the new equilibrium quantity (point R) a total expenditure which exceeds the payment demanded by sellers by precisely the amount of the tax (RR′ = TT′). With convex indifference curves, Q lies on a higher indifference curve than does R.

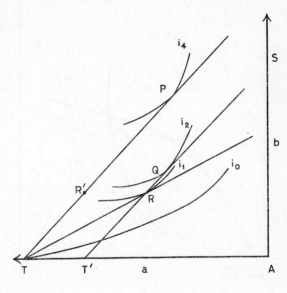

FIG 3a

The above interpretation of Fig. 3a applies to partial equilibrium analysis: an individual is buying in an open market at prices given from outside the system considered. We can, however, supplement the diagram by adding a second party with origin at B and indifference curves j_0, j_1, j_2 . . . (Fig. 3b). Individual B now holds BT of commodity b. Individual A holds AT of commodity a.

The individuals are free to exchange. The locus BPA of points of tangency between i curves and j curves is the locus of efficient points. The model now depicts in

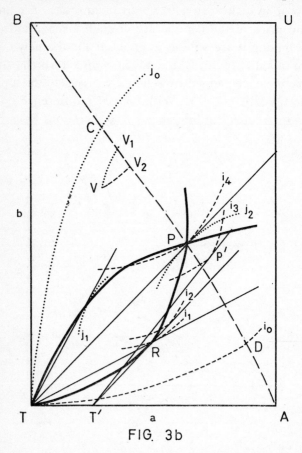

FIG. 3b

principle a closed economy. If the individuals are competitors in a barter economy, trading under conditions of passive price adjustment ('competitive behaviour') equilibrium is at P. (If they are bilateral monopolists, equilibrium is somewhere in the range CD.) The general equilibrium solution requires, in addition to the condition of equality of substitution rates required for partial equilibrium, the further condition that the total amount offered of each commodity used should equal the total amount demanded.

The removal by the government of specified amounts of *a* and *b* collected by a price tax implies imposing differential prices for the two persons A and B, such that the supply of each commodity exceeds the demand for it by the said specified amounts. The geometrical representation of this

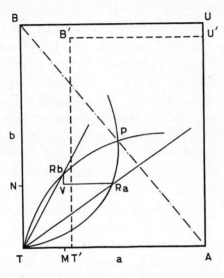

FIG. 3c

was given by A. P. Lerner.[1] The reciprocal demand of each party is illustrated by an offer curve and the position of each party by some point on its offer curve. The equilibrium pair of prices for the two respective parties is that pair, say $\dfrac{R_aN}{TN}$ and $\dfrac{TM}{R_bM}$ in Fig. 3c, which makes the excess offers of *a* and *b* (horizontal and vertical distances between the points R_a and R_b) equal to the levies of *a* and *b* to be raised by the government.[2] The required *ad*

---

[1] 'Symmetry of Import and Export Duties', *Economica*, August 1936.
[2] There may be more than one such pair of prices.

valorem tax is determined by the relation between these prices. The equilibrium positions of A and B, R_a and R_b respectively, both lie off the efficient locus APB.

If now the government raises the same amounts R_aV of a, R_bV of b, by direct levies in kind this may be depicted by reducing the sides of the box TAUB by the amounts of the levy so that the economy, after tax, is represented by the reduced box T'AU'B'. If the two parties are allowed, within this reduced economy, to exchange freely, this will, under competitive behaviour, lead to the establishment of a single price and to quantities consumed (and exchanged) which are efficient. That is, it will lead to equilibrium on the contract locus running from A to B'. Provided that in the final equilibrium the price lies between the upper and lower prices established under the alternative system of taxing, each party will (as in the partial equilibrium case) end up on a higher indifference curve than he does under that alternative system. The new equilibrium price will, in general, differ from the equilibrium price prior to taxation and the new equilibrium will be at some point like P' in Fig. 3b. This illustration tells us nothing — as it should tell us nothing — about whether it is better to make individual A or B or both pay the levy.

The diagram may be used still more generally. It may be regarded as depicting the distribution of 'goods' (whether producer goods or consumer goods) between 'users' (whether industries or persons). The two sides of the box depict the total amounts of the two kinds of goods. The initial distribution of these goods — which might, for instance, represent the allocation by Robinson Crusoe of prime factors between two industries — might be anywhere in the box, say, at V in Fig. 3b. At such a point allocation is sub-optimal. Movement towards $V_1 V_2$ where factor substitution rates are equal, is an improvement. The diagram does not tell us — as it should not tell us, since this must depend upon demand conditions — what point between $V_1 V_2$ is best.

The inefficiency of taxes other than those in kind which shows up graphically in the creation of equilibria off the efficiency curve, shows up in the matrix by the unequal substitution rates in different parts of the matrix and in differences between the optimal and the actual intensities in each activity. Such divergences denote inefficiency whether they arise in respect of consumer activities (deviation from the contract curve in Marshall's barter diagram) or in respect of producer activities (deviation from the Samuelson-Stolper production contract curve in a production economy with or without exchange). Lerner's identity of imposts levied on imports and exports, all other things being equal, would emerge immediately from the matrix formulation, as it must from any general equilibrium formulation, since the distinction between 'import' and 'export' disappears: they are two sides of the activity of exchange.

Limitations of the Analysis

The above analysis of the effect of different forms of tax has, with the exception of the geometrical constructions 3b and 3c, referred wholly to a one-man economy. Clearly the principles of taxation in which we are interested are those which apply to nations, not to Robinson Crusoe's island. Is our analysis capable of extension to communities? From certain points of view the analysis is applicable to communities. The principle established, that levies in kind are the only sort of tax which avoids (except by coincidence) shifts away from the optimal allocation arrangement for meeting both the consumer's desires and the government's tax, is valid regardless of the number of individuals. When we take into account the multiplicity of individuals, a new question does indeed arise. If taxes must be levied in kind, they must be levied from the people who have or can produce the particular goods in question. This is likely to cut right across our ethical views upon the proper distribution of the tax burden — indeed the *raison d'être* of much taxation is redistribution of wealth in a particular direction. What would be the good of raising a lot of resources efficiently from the wrong individuals? The pursuit of this topic would raise some interesting points, but it would almost inevitably involve us deeply in the concept of 'community welfare' and inter-personal comparison of utility. These are questions which cannot be handled in this book.

We shall therefore meet the question we have raised only by a brief suggestion : if and when we can really define what is to be maximized in the community (the 'welfare function' if you like) then probably the canon of efficiency in taxation would require us to separate into two operations *tax raising* and *income-redistribution*.

We have said that the principle established in our Robinson Crusoe example of wasteful secondary shifts in allocation of resources as a result of inefficient forms of tax, does have application in a community. The fact that we have chosen to demonstrate the waste in a model for a one-man economy is, however, not an accident. The first difficulty about carrying through the analysis for a group of people is that we should have to be able to make inter-personal comparisons of welfare — there must be a maximand if there is to be any solution. Now this is not a limitation of the techniques used here. It applies quite generally to analysis in any terms of 'efficient' and 'inefficient' systems of taxation as soon as the possibility of shifts in distribution of income is allowed to enter.

Even if we eliminated this difficulty by assuming that

we do measure and compare the utilities of all the individuals in the economy (however arbitrary the procedure) we would come up against a second one : that of representing, in the matrix formulation, exchange within the economy.

CHAPTER IX

THE PURE THEORY OF SPECIALIZATION

Introductory

IT has been seen that taxes other then levies in kind carry with them loss of efficiency through entailing a non-optimal allocation of resources characterized by unequal substitution rates in different parts of the system. Taxation is, however, not the only thing which may give rise to such non-optimal allocation of resources. Differences in owner-ship, for instance, may give rise to it. As soon as available resources are controlled by more than one person there is no guarantee that the different owners will act so as to obtain the maximum from the total of their joint resources. More generally, non-optimal allocation may arise from the fact that economic activity is undertaken by units of control, and the free allocation between the different units may be hindered by taxes and other barriers. This leads us to consider the role of specialization in equilibrium theory. To fix ideas, we shall suppose that the different units are geographical areas.

The Pure Theory of Specialization in Production with Two Production Areas and a Single Consumer

Suppose that there are two producing areas, both with the same known techniques, and a single consumption activity (Table 29).

	ACTIVITIES				RESOURCES
	PRODUCTION			CON-SUMPTION	
	AREA I		AREA II		
	I	II	III	IV	V	
ut 1 in Area 1	-5	-1	0	0	0	$\geqslant -105$
ut 2 in Area 1	-1	-4	0	0	0	$\geqslant -40$
ut 1 in Area 2	0	0	-5	-1	0	$\geqslant -39$
ut 2 in Area 2	0	0	-1	-4	0	$\geqslant -80$
put 1	1	0	1	0	-1	$\geqslant$ 0
put 2	0	1	0	1	-1	$\geqslant$ 0
tility index	0	0	0	0	5	Max.

TABLE 29

The optimal solution, where the x's refer to the level of intensity in each of the five activities respectively, is:

$$x_1 = 20$$
$$x_2 = 5$$
$$x_3 = 4$$
$$x_4 = 19$$
$$x_5 = 24.$$

In such a case neither area taken separately produces the required consumption pattern, while taken together the two areas do so. We say, therefore, that there is regional 'specialization'.

If now for any reason free allocation is not possible, i.e. 'specialization' is not possible between the two locations, the optimal solution is:

Area I	*Area II*
$x_1' = x_2' = x_5' = 8$	$x_3'' = x_4'' = x_5'' = 6\frac{1}{2}$

where the x's refer to the equilibrium intensities of production and consumption activities in each area. Since there is unused Input 1 in Area I and unused Input 2 in Area II, and substitution rates are different in the two areas, there would be gain through specialization. As is seen from the solutions, the index of total utility is 120 with specialization, and $72\frac{1}{2}$ in the absence of it.

Given a common utility function and identical known techniques throughout the system, the possibility of gain through specialization depends simply upon whether the prime resources are available in different proportions in the two areas. If this proportion is identical, specialization brings no gain ; if it varies between the areas, specialization brings gain.

Geometrically, the situation is illustrated in Figs. 4

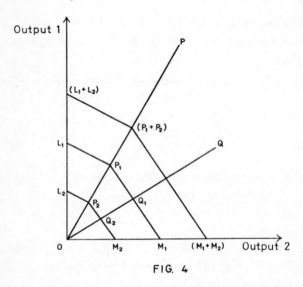

FIG. 4

and 5. Here the production possibility boundary for Area I is shown as $L_1P_1M_1$, where P_1 is the point of intersection of the two constraining lines for the two factors. That is, P_1 is the kink of Area I's boundary. Similarly, the production possibility boundary for Area II is shown as $L_2P_2M_2$, where P_2 is the point of intersection of the two constraining lines for the two factors. That is, P_2 is the

kink of Area II's boundary. Given the same known
techniques, the production boundary for the whole area
taken together coincides with, or lies outside, the sum of
the separate production boundaries according to whether

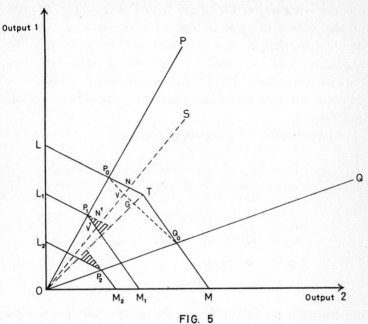

FIG. 5

the factor proportions of the two areas are the same or
different. If the factor proportions of the areas are the
same, the kinks (P_1 and P_2) must lie on the same radial, as
in Fig. 4. In this case, the co-ordinates of the joint
production boundary are simply the sum of the co-
ordinates of the separate production boundaries of the two
areas, for any given output pattern. In other words there
can be no gain from specialization between the two areas.
If the factor proportions of the two areas differ, the kink
P_I must be on a different radial from the kink P_2, as in
Fig. 5. In this case the co-ordinates of the joint production boundary, for any output pattern lying between

A.A.—H

those denoted by the radials OP_1 and OP_2 respectively, exceed the sum of the co-ordinates of the separate production boundaries of the two areas. The latter is given by the boundary LP_0VGQ_0M, where P_0VGQ_0 is a curve lying nearer the origin than P_0TQ_0. The amount of the excess of joint output over the sum of the individual outputs is also indicated in Fig. 5 by the line segment [1] $V'N'$ for the consumption pattern OS, and the corresponding line segments (drawn in but not lettered) for each other consumption pattern between OP and OQ.[2]

Algebraically, for a matrix of the form

$-a_{11}$	$-a_{12}$	0	0	0	$\geqslant -b_1$
$-a_{21}$	$-a_{22}$	0	0	0	$\geqslant -b_2$
0	0	$-a_{11}$	$-a_{12}$	0	$\geqslant -b_3$
0	0	$-a_{21}$	$-a_{22}$	0	$\geqslant -b_4$
a_{51}	a_{52}	a_{51}	a_{52}	$-a_{55}$	$\geqslant$ 0
a_{61}	a_{62}	a_{61}	a_{62}	$-a_{65}$	$\geqslant$ 0
0	0	0	0	c	Max.

TABLE 30

the co-ordinates of the intercepts of the boundaries with the axes, assuming the columns are so arranged that $\dfrac{a_{11}}{a_{21}} > \dfrac{a_{12}}{a_{22}}$, are given by $\dfrac{b_1}{a_{11}}$; $\dfrac{b_2}{a_{22}}$ for Area I and $\dfrac{b_3}{a_{11}}$; $\dfrac{b_4}{a_{22}}$ for Area II.

A necessary condition for gain through specialization is:

$$\frac{\dfrac{b_1}{a_{11}}}{\dfrac{b_3}{a_{11}}} \neq \frac{\dfrac{b_2}{a_{22}}}{\dfrac{b_4}{a_{22}}} \qquad \text{or} \qquad \frac{b_1}{b_2} \neq \frac{b_3}{b_4},$$

i.e. different proportions between effectively scarce factors

---

[1] The point N' lies on L_1P_1 produced. $V'N' = VN$.
[2] See Geometrical Appendix to Chapter IX.

in the two areas. The condition $\frac{b_1}{b_2} \neq \frac{b_3}{b_4}$ corresponds to the geometrical condition that the radial going through OP_1 does not coincide with the radial going through OP_2.

Whatever the number of factors, a necessary condition for gain from specialization remains: a variation, as between the different sources, in the endowments of factors which are *effectively* scarce (over the relevant range of activities). There is no gain from specialization if any line drawn from the centre to the outer boundary passes through successive area boundaries at the same angle, or at a corner having the same two slopes. The boundaries may also be drawn continuously and the condition for zero gain from specialization is seen to be the familiar one that the function describing production opportunities for two areas should be a homogeneous one; but in the present model — where available techniques are assumed the same in the two areas — this homogeneous condition is seen to mean simply the equality of factor endowment ratios.

The above applies to any number of areas with any number of factors and outputs.

Given the same known techniques and a single consumption activity, differing factor proportions are thus a necessary condition for gain from specialization, but they are not a sufficient one. Obviously technical coefficients must also be variable; and the extent of the gain will be influenced by other factors.

Suppose production conditions as in Table 31 below. This represents two areas, the same techniques available in both areas, joint inputs, no jointness in outputs.

If b_1, b_2, b_3, and b_4 are all given, this means that both the overall resources and the resources in each area are given.

AREA I		AREA II		RESOURCES
I	II	I	II	
$-a_{11}$	$-a_{12}$	0	0	$\geqslant -b_1$
$-a_{21}$	$-a_{22}$	0	0	$\geqslant -b_2$
0	0	$-a_{11}$	$-a_{12}$	$\geqslant -b_3$
0	0	$-a_{21}$	$-a_{22}$	$\geqslant -b_4$
a_{51}	0	a_{51}	0	$\geqslant 0$
0	a_{62}	0	a_{62}	$\geqslant 0$

Max.

TABLE 31

What factors govern the magnitude of the gain from specialization ? In our present simple model a simple answer can be given. It can be proven [1] that the gain from specialization is greater :

(1) The greater the angle POQ, i.e. the greater the difference in slopes OP and OQ, i.e. the greater the difference between $\dfrac{OL_1}{OM_1}$ and $\dfrac{OL_2}{OM_2}$ (Fig. 5). If the angle POQ is increased while all other things are kept equal, the length VN increases.

In terms of algebra (Table 31) specialization brings more gain the less similar the ratio of the boundaries $\left(\dfrac{b_1}{b_3} \text{ and } \dfrac{b_2}{b_4}\right)$ in the two areas.

In economic terms, specialization brings more gain the less similar are the factor proportions in the two areas.

(2) The greater the difference in the slopes of LT and TM, i.e. the less the angle LTM. If this angle is reduced while other things are kept equal, the length VN increases.

In terms of algebra, specialization brings more gain the less similar are the production activities, i.e. the less similar are the ratios $\dfrac{a_{11}}{a_{21}}$ and $\dfrac{a_{12}}{a_{22}}$.

In economic terms, specialization brings more gain the less similar are the technical coefficients of production in the two activities.

[1] See Geometrical Appendix to Chapter IX.

(3) The more closely the relative size of two areas for any *given* total output in the absence of specialization approaches the optimal ratio. This optimal ratio is that which results in the kink of the joint boundary lying on the same radial through the origin (i.e. having the same output pattern) as does the given total output in the absence of specialization.

In terms of the matrix, specialization brings more gain the more nearly $\dfrac{b_1}{b_3}$ $\left(\text{or } \dfrac{b_2}{b_4}\right)$ approximates to a certain optimal value.

In economic terms, gain from specialization is greater the more nearly the relative size of the two areas approaches the 'critical balance'. No simple definition of this can be given, but the meaning is that, given the factor endowment ratio that characterizes each area, the two areas must be so balanced in size as to allow of the maximum amount of specialization in both, before either area reaches 'complete specialization' so far as its favourable-cost activity is concerned.

The Influence of Tastes on the Gain from Specialization of Production, with a Single Consumer

We have seen that the gain from specialization in production for any given consumption pattern is greater the less similar are the areas in factor endowments and comparative costs and the more appropriately balanced they are in size. In this discussion we have abstracted from taste conditions, simply treating the equilibrium pattern of output as a datum. In fact, it is part of the solution of the problem under examination, and it results from the interaction of the production factors we have been discussing with the consumption factors, which we have omitted from consideration. We turn now to consider the consumption side (consumer activities).

In our present problem we are examining a single

consumer with two production locations. We have, therefore, to consider how the tastes of this individual may
influence the equilibrium pattern of output. It is at once
obvious that if tastes are such as to place output in both
areas under conditions of separate production, at points
above OP (Fig. 5), there can be no gain from joint production (specialization). Similarly, if under conditions of
separate activities tastes are such as to lead to production
at points below OQ, there can be no gain from specialization. In either of such cases equilibrium is outside the
zone of gains from specialization : there is no difference in
comparative costs between the areas.

Conversely, if tastes are such as to place output in both
areas, when acting separately, within the area POQ then
(so long as there is only one taste function in the system)
specialization must bring some gain. The gain will be
small if equilibrium output is near the limit OP or OQ ;
between these limits lies that output pattern for which
gain from specialization is at a maximum.

If the tastes function is homogeneous the equilibrium
outputs under isolated activities in the two areas must
either both be above OP, or both below OQ, or both
between them. (If the restriction to a homogeneous taste
function is removed, the isolated equilibrium positions
might be anywhere in the whole space, and gain from
specialization may arise in all cases except where the
isolated equilibria both lie above OP or below OQ.)

Given all the production factors, the gain from specialization must, therefore, be greater the more closely taste
conditions conform to the pattern which will yield the
particular equilibrium output corresponding to maximum
specialization gain. If there is only one consumption
activity and this specifies outputs in precisely that ratio
which permits maximum gain from specialization in production, then tastes permit the realization of the maximum

potential gain made possible by production conditions. But this is too narrow a restriction to place upon consumption activities : the maximum potential gain may also be achieved if different consumption activities are used in equilibrium in the two areas acting in isolation, provided that the combination of these different activities gives the output ratio permitting maximum potential gain from specialization in production as a whole.[1]

The Pure Theory of Specialization in Consumption

So far we have analysed gain from specialization in production in a Robinson Crusoe economy. We used the model of a one-man economy, with two separate production units — two plantations on Crusoe's island. This abstraction is only of interest as a step towards an analysis of the gains of specialization in a world of many people and nations ; it enables us to distinguish the main factors at work on the production side while treating the consumption factors as 'given'. We have, however, in the preceding paragraph led off into the analysis of the role of the consumption factors by considering the case where Crusoe has more than one consumption activity : in principle, he has a (homogeneous) Preference system. The analysis may now be extended to the case where there is more than one consumption activity which pertains to more than one consumer.

We reverse the procedure followed above. We subsume production conditions and focus attention on consumption conditions. We postulate two consumers, but

[1] It may be noted in this connection that once all the factors on the production side are given, the similarity or dissimilarity of the pattern of quantities actually consumed (and produced) in the two areas is in itself irrelevant to the size of gain to be secured from specialization — except in the sense that one way of having that *total* output ratio which yields the full potential gain is to have this ratio obtaining in each of the areas when operating in isolation.

we abstract from the multiplicity of production activities and postulate only one. To keep our matrix formally correct we have added four 'distribution activities' which mean that when there is specialization, production for the first consumer can be costlessly allocated to the second consumer and *vice versa*. We have shown three consumption activities for each consumer, giving two line-segments of each consumer's indifference boundary. We shall also suppose that the output bundles open to consumers are the *same* for both consumers. These conditions are depicted in Table 32.

Fig. 6 gives a geometrical illustration of such a matrix. Suppose that, for consumption activities involving product proportions outside the lowest and highest proportions in

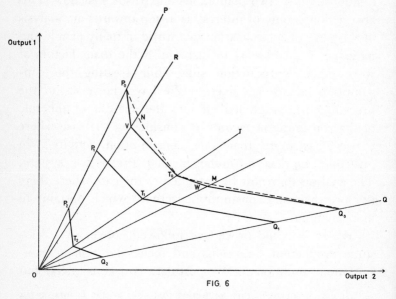

FIG. 6

the matrix, the two consumers have identical consumption activities (i.e. identical in respect to both *a*-coefficients and *c*-coefficients). Within the ratios given in the matrix, consumption activities may differ for the two consumers.

TABLE 32

| | Activities | | | | | | | | | | | | Resources |
| | Production | | Distribution | | | | Consumption | | | | | | |
	I	II	III	IV	V	VI	VII	VIII	IX	X	XI	XII	
Input of Consumer I	$-a_{11}$	0	0	0	0	0	0	0	0	0	0	0	$\geqq -b_1$
Input of Consumer II	0	$-a_{22}$	0	0	0	0	0	0	0	0	0	0	$\geqq -b_2$
Output 1 of Consumer I	a_{31}	0	-1	0	1	0	$-a_{37}$	$-a_{38}$	$-a_{39}$	0	0	0	$\geqq 0$
Output 2 of Consumer I	a_{41}	0	0	-1	0	1	$-a_{47}$	$-a_{48}$	$-a_{49}$	0	0	0	$\geqq 0$
Output 1 of Consumer II	0	a_{31}	1	0	-1	0	0	0	0	$-a_{37}$	$-a_{38}$	$-a_{39}$	$\geqq 0$
Output 2 of Consumer II	0	a_{41}	0	1	0	-1	0	0	0	$-a_{47}$	$-a_{48}$	$-a_{49}$	$\geqq 0$
Utility	0	0	0	0	0	0	c_7	c_8	c_9	c_{10}	c_{11}	c_{12}	Max.

The lowest and highest ratios are indicated in Fig. 6 by OQ and OP. Along any radial below OQ or above OP we assume that the slope of any indifference boundary of the first consumer and of the second consumer are the same.[1]

A segment of an indifference curve of the first consumer is shown by $P_1 T_1 Q_1$; and a segment of an indifference curve of the second consumer by $P_2 T_2 Q_2$. The level of consumption is in each case determined by production. We may suppose that the magnitude of production by each consumer acting separately is such that in equilibrium Consumer I can reach the locus $P_1 T_1 Q_1$ and Consumer II can reach $P_2 T_2 Q_2$. The sum of the separate consumption amounts, for any given output pattern, say OR, is found by summing the co-ordinates of the points at which that radial cuts $P_1 T_1 Q_1$ and $P_2 T_2 Q_2$ respectively. The locus of total consumption quantities which, in the absence of specialization in consumption, will give each consumer the level of satisfaction attaching to the boundaries $P_1 T_1 Q_1$ and $P_2 T_2 Q_2$ respectively, is shown as $P_0 N T_0 M Q_0$. The locus of total consumption quantities which can yield these levels of satisfaction if specialization in consumption is introduced, is shown by $P_0 V T_0 W Q_0$. This boundary may be plotted by drawing successively, from the point Q_0 (which is the sum of the separate co-ordinates Q_1 and Q_2), the line segments $Q_1 T_1$, $Q_2 T_2$, $T_1 P_1$, and $T_2 P_2$. It lies nearer the origin than does $P_0 N T_0 M Q_0$.

Given the conditions depicted, it may be seen that the gain from specialization depends upon there being a difference in the slopes of the two consumer boundaries. For clarity, we may confine our attention to cases where production conditions are such that the output pattern lies

[1] Since OQ may coincide with the horizontal axis, and OP with the vertical axis, this assumption is not as restrictive as it may seem at first sight. But it does suppose that, if the two consumers' indifference curves are similar for any pattern of output, this occurs for extreme patterns. If one assumes, on the contrary, similarity for the middle ranges of output combinations, and dissimilarity for the extremes, the geometry would be different.

somewhere above or upon OT (the argument may be applied *mutatis mutandis* to cases where it lies below OT). Then:

(1) The greater the difference in the slopes of P_1T_1 and P_2T_2, the greater the gain from specialization, for any given output pattern.

In terms of algebra (Table 32), if the technology or a-coefficients are identical for the two consumers, then the gain from specialization is greater the more the ratios $\dfrac{c_8}{c_7}$ and $\dfrac{c_{11}}{c_{12}}$ differ.

In economic terms, the gain from specialization is greater the greater the divergence between the two consumers' relative evaluations of the pair of activities in question.

(2) Given the difference between the slopes of P_1T_1 and P_2T_2, the gain from specialization is greater, the greater the divergence between OT and OP, that is, the greater the angle POT.

In terms of algebra, the gain from specialization is greater the greater the difference between the ratio of the coefficients in the two activities, that is, the more $\dfrac{a_{37}}{a_{47}}$ differs from $\dfrac{a_{38}}{a_{48}}$.

In terms of economics, the gain from specialization is greater the less similar are the consumer activities.

(3) Given all the slopes of the indifference curves and the slopes of OP and OQ, the extent of the gain from specialization depends upon the relative sizes of the outputs consumed by the two consumers in isolation. If we take as given that the consumption pattern in isolation is that denoted by the radial OR, and that the sum of the quantities consumed by both consumers in isolation is ON, what relative magnitudes for the separate consumers imply the possibility of the greatest gain from specialization? This

may be examined by using a procedure analogous to that adopted earlier to determine the optimum relative size for two producing areas with different factor endowments. If we suppose that the entire consumption ON belongs to the first consumer, then there can be no gain from specialization in consumption. The joint indifference boundary and the individual indifference boundary coincide at all points, including the point N. As we reduce the level of the first consumer's consumption below ON, we have to impute a corresponding positive consumption to the second consumer to maintain the condition that the sum of isolated consumption bundles is given by ON. There is one value for the ratio of the consumption of the two individuals which maximizes the gain from specialization. In the assumed conditions this may be found geometrically by finding that pair of individual boundaries P_1T_1 and P_2T_2 such that the parallelogram which may be formed from the two sides P_1O and OT_2 has its corner (opposite to the corner at O) on the radial OR as in Fig. 6. In terms of the variables in Table 32 the nearer $\dfrac{b_1}{b_2}$ approximates to the optimal value, the greater the gain from specialization in consumption.

In economic terms, specialization gain is greater the more nearly the ratio between the outputs of the two individual consumers approaches that value which permits the maximum amount of specialization in consumption, before either reaches complete specialization in respect of its favourable consumption activity.

The Influence of Production on the Gain from Specialization in Consumption, with a Single Production Source

The above summarizes the factors on the tastes side which govern the magnitude of the advantage that is to be derived from 'specialization' in consumption, assuming any given equilibrium pattern of output. In fact, the latter is part of the solution of the problem, depending upon production and consumption factors. Among the factors on the consumption side is the *weighting of individual utilities*. The final equilibrium can only be determined in the system assumed here if weights are attached to each individual's final evaluations.

The Pure Theory of Specialization in Production and Consumption with two Parties

We have examined successively the gains from specialization with respect to production, assuming a single rigidly fixed consumption ratio and the gains from specialization with respect to consumption, assuming a single rigidly fixed production ratio. Either assumption implies a very special or limiting case, where substitutability (either in consumption or in production) is zero. To get more generally valid results simultaneous consideration of both production and consumption conditions would be necessary. There are a large number of ways in which they may be combined.

The reader will have noticed that the two successive constructions used above are designed so as to cut out of the problem any need for a theory of exchange and the balance of payments. The first exercise was based upon a one-man economy or at least a uniform consumer preference function. The second was again a sort of communist economy, inasmuch as the given production possibilities of the economy were directed towards satisfying the two consumers' needs according to priorities dictated from outside. There was no link between any one consumer and a part of the production resources, no question of a consumer having to balance his consumption by his production and export, under conditions of specialization.

The Theory of Regional Customs Unions or Alternative Tariff Structures (*the Theory of Specialization with more than Two Parties*)

The above analysis of the factors governing the size of gains from specialization has an application to any economy incorporating more than one production unit and/or more than one consumption unit. Large firms owning a number of different factories and/or supplying a number of different markets ought (in theory) to want to know how optimally to integrate their various units' activities. The different 'units' may be defined in many ways — e.g. one might be staffed by men, and another by women, etc., etc. — and the theory we are developing about the interaction of different units in an economy may be thought of quite generally as the theory of economic grouping. But an obviously important kind of demarcation between units is by reference to location : enterprises in different places are different units. It is, of course, primarily this characteristic that we have had in mind in labouring the above analysis ; and we have been interested in spatial specialization primarily because of its importance with reference to international trade. The elaborate analysis has not, however, been undertaken with a view to revealing the gains from *laisser faire* and *laisser passer*. That free trade throughout the world brings more efficient production to the world is a proposition which, while true, has no great interest for research (because it has long since been clearly established) and perhaps less importance in practice than a slightly different proposition. In practice the policy alternatives between which Presidents of the Board of Trade, or conferences of Prime Ministers, seem actually to choose are not world free trade or protection, but rather this or that pattern of economic alliance (e.g. Commonwealth Preference or European Customs Union).

In other words, at the present stage of affairs trade policies run largely along the lines of regional systems, not a universal system, of trade. Such systems may be customs unions, or federations, or much looser preferential agreements. In what follows we shall consider only complete customs unions (involving zero tariffs between members). Moreover, we shall assume that the absence of a union is accompanied by the imposition of *prohibitive* tariffs throughout. This latter is very unrealistic; but non-prohibitive tariffs mean simultaneously a reduction of specialization gain *and also* price distortion. Analytically, it is desirable to keep these two elements distinct; and the latter has been dealt with already (under an even more unrealistic isolating device) in Chapter VIII.

Our problem then is to consider which of given alternative systems of regional customs unions is more efficient. The answer to this is largely contained in the preceding paragraphs. For any given country, we may find the optimal partner by finding the specialization gain for each alternative partner, and seeing which partner gives the biggest joint gain.[1] And this gain will be larger the greater the difference in natural resources of the two areas, the greater the difference in tastes,[2] the greater the variation in production methods used in the two countries, the more rigid the patterns of consumption, and the more equally balanced the partners are in magnitude.

So far we have been concerned with the question: what type of region should a given country choose for forming a customs union, in order that the greatest gain

---

[1] It is tacitly assumed that if the joint gain is biggest our particular country's gain is also biggest — in other words, we do not attempt to introduce differential bargaining power.

[2] Although it is possible to construct examples where differences on the resources and on the tastes side offset each other, thus reducing or eliminating the gain.

should be secured in its customs area? This, however, still does not give the answer to the question: what system of regional customs unions is best for the world as a whole? As has been said above, world trade today approximates neither to the system of universal free trade, nor to the situation where one customs union area is formed among a lot of countries acting on their own. Rather, countries range themselves into groups, forming a number of 'regions' (not necessarily contiguous) within which trade is (more or less) free and between which trade is (more or less) cut off. One might say that it is the way in which the membership of these regions is to be composed which constitutes the subject of many current negotiations and debates on international trade.

Now if this is what is in fact happening, we need to know what the alternative groupings are — e.g. (a) the British Commonwealth; Europe; the U.S.A. and S. America; the Iron Curtain Countries; or (b) Britain and Western Europe; Eastern Europe including U.S.S.R.; the Western Hemisphere; Asia and Australasia, etc., etc. But one general point may be made: if the world has got to be cut up into (say) four regions for trading purposes, there are good and bad ways of doing the quartering, from the world's point of view. And it is quite possible that a grouping which brings large gain in one customs union area is not optimal for the world as a whole. Such a case, for an example of four countries which are to form two groups, may be illustrated as follows. We take a very simple case of a single technical production function producing outputs in a fixed proportion, equivalent to a single commodity. Let the activity matrices, with differing factor endowments and fixed and similar consumption pattern for four countries, be as in Table 33. Maximum output with isolated production is 1 in A, 2 in B, $\frac{1}{2}$ in C, and $\frac{1}{2}$ in D.

A		B		C		D	
-1	$\geqslant -4$	-1	$\geqslant -2$	-1	$\geqslant -\frac{1}{2}$	-1	$\geqslant -\frac{1}{2}$
-1	$\geqslant -1$	-1	$\geqslant -4$	-1	$\geqslant -1$	-1	$\geqslant -5$
1		1		1		1	

TABLE 33

There are three possible ways of forming the four countries into two customs regions, each comprising two countries. The total outputs, and the joint gain from specialization in each customs region, under each alternative, are as follows:

CUSTOMS REGIONS

	(i) AB and CD		(ii) AC and BD		(iii) AD and BC	
Total output in isolation	3	1	$1\frac{1}{2}$	$2\frac{1}{2}$	$1\frac{1}{2}$	$2\frac{1}{2}$
Total joint output	5	1	2	$2\frac{1}{2}$	$4\frac{1}{2}$	$2\frac{1}{2}$
Joint gain from specialization	2	0	$\frac{1}{2}$	0	3	0

TABLE 34

From the point of view of B, alternative (i) offers the greatest gain from trade. From the point of view of the world, alternative (iii) is better. (This, in fact, is as good as world free trade.) From the point of view of C, (ii) is best.

We are able to reach such a simple conclusion only because we have taken the highly special case of a fixed bundle of consumption throughout the world, which is equivalent to a single output. We have further assumed that the utility of a unit of consumption is the same in all countries. If these restrictions are raised we at once lose our simple maximand, and we are left with the problem of 'Community Welfare'.

The Restricting Assumptions

We have reached the conclusion that the gain to be derived from production specialization by the individual

A.A.—I

economic units is greater the more the proportions in which the prime factors are available vary as between the units, the more the technical coefficients of production vary as between the different processes of production, and the more closely 'matched' in size are the units. Correspondingly on the consumption side the potential gain from specialization is greater the greater the difference in activity evaluations as between units, the greater the differences in the coefficients in the different consumer activities, and the more closely 'matched' in size are the units. These conclusions have, however, been reached only by dint of adopting a particular explicit model of the economic system. How far are our conclusions limited to this particular special case ? And how special is the case ?

The main simplifying features of the model upon which the conclusions of this chapter have been based are as follows: that there are not more than two outputs and two factors of production in each economic unit; that the same techniques are known to all units; that output from any given production activity is independent of the scale upon which that activity is carried on; that the consumer's relative utility from any given type of consumption activity is independent of the scale upon which that activity is carried on; that the weighting of different consumers' utility is given from outside; and, in some cases, that outputs are not joint. These restrictions vary all the way from the harmless to the ridiculous, and entail widely differing kinds of implications.

Some of the simplifications are a mere expositional convenience and can be removed without complicating the main conclusions. Other simplifications are directly responsible for the simple terms in which the conclusions run, and the generalization of the model in these aspects would necessarily entail a loss of simplicity in the conclusions. Finally, some of our assumptions imply things about the real world which may be either true or untrue — and which will probably strike the reader as the latter.

The assumption of absence of jointness in outputs (Tables 29 and 31) has been made for convenience of exposition, and may be removed with no effects upon the analysis other than an increase in clumsiness. The restriction of two prime factors and two kinds of consumer goods is more fundamental. With this restriction 'similarity of factor endowment ratios' and 'similarity of consumption patterns', 'similarity of production coefficients', and 'similarity of coefficients in consumer activities' have a simple measurable interpretation (reflected in the angles and slopes of the geometrical illustrations). When we abandon this very special case, we have to recognize that relative factor endowments, final utility evaluations, production coefficients, and consumption coefficients each become a vector instead of a single variable. The simple concept of 'factor ratio' must be replaced by a set of ratios, and so on. It is clear that the notion of economies being similar or complementary in respect of endowments, techniques, or tastes becomes correspondingly less simple. Although in some cases such a classification may still be unambiguously made, in others this may not be so.[1] It follows that the attempt in this chapter to deduce characteristics of the system which determine the size of the gain from international trade (or more generally the gain from specialization) still refers, in spite of its heavy complexity, to cases which are in an important sense special cases.

The assumption that the same techniques are known to all the different economic units in the system must, again, be questioned on the ground of its lack of correspondence with empirical facts. It may well appear to be a

---

[1] See H. Makower and G. Morton, 'Contribution towards a Theory of Customs Unions', *Economic Journal*, March 1953, p. 35.

misleading assumption, especially in its implications for foreign trade problems. For would we not expect that undeveloped countries (with their factor endowment contrasting with that of industrial countries) would have undeveloped techniques ? This may be so. It is quite easy to incorporate such differences in our matrices and diagrams (the latter will then show varying slopes at every point on the production boundary for the two countries, rather than two slopes which are in themselves the same for both countries but apply over different ranges). However, such a further elaboration of the model (modification of our A-matrix) would appear to point to different general conclusions only if we were to introduce important differences in known techniques as between countries with *similar* factor endowments. Such differences obviously do exist ; but it seems doubtful whether they are characteristic of the situation. One would expect that industrial countries with the same sort of resources would tend to get to know the best techniques and use them. In so far as known techniques differ rather between differently endowed countries than between countries with similar endowments, the conclusion that difference in factor endowment is (assuming the same tastes) a fundamental condition for any gain from trade remains valid.

A similar point arises on the demand side : backward areas may have no knowledge of sophisticated types of consumption of goods never produced in their economies ; but if a modern industrial country started to produce goods for export to sophisticated consumers over the frontier, how long would the consumers in the exporting country remain unaware of this type of consumption ? The idea that they would do so seems unreal : more than that, unlike the situation on the resources side, where physical conditions determine the basic availabilities in the different countries, final utility evaluations are less fixed, and, in fact, are probably infectious.[1] This means that not only is it unlikely that differences in the co-efficients inside the A-matrix for consumer activities vary greatly as between closely connected economies, but also the c boundaries may tend to become equal. This gives still more weight to factor endowment as the principal source of gain from trade.

The idea that much good could be done by encouraging an expanded two-way trade in refined manufactures between such similar economies as, say, Belgium and Germany almost seems to imply that Belgium would think up new tempting consumer goods and export them to Germany, while Germany thought up different ones for export to Belgium, although both of them would be able to supply the other's exports at the same cost, and to sell them for the same price, at home.

The question of interpersonal (inter-unit, international) comparisons of utility has been evaded and begged throughout, in conformity with a long tradition in handling this difficulty. The significance of the assumption of 'constant returns' in respect of any given activity has been discussed at length in Chapter VI.

[1] See R. Nurkse, *Problems of Capital Formation*, p. 58, and J. S. Duesenberry, *Income, Saving and the Theory of Consumer Behaviour*.

PART 3

INTERDEPENDENCE IN THE ECONOMIC SYSTEM

CHAPTER X

FUNDAMENTAL FEATURES OF COMPARATIVE STATICS ANALYSIS IN ECONOMICS

Fundamental Structure of an Economy

THE fundamental structure of a production economy, as we have been depicting it, is reproduced in Table 35. It schematizes the Technology (first three columns inside the matrix), the Tastes (last three columns inside the matrix together with c boundaries), and Resources (b boundaries to the right-hand side of the last column). Thus the A-matrix, the b's, and the c's are the data.

		ACTIVITIES					RESOURCES
		PRODUCTION			CONSUMPTION		
		I	II	III	IV	V	VI	
	Intensities :	x_1	x_2	x_3	x_4	x_5	x_6	
Internal Prices y_1		$-a_{11}$	$-a_{12}$	$-a_{13}$	o	o	o	$\geqslant -b_1$
y_2		$-a_{21}$	$-a_{22}$	$-a_{23}$	o	o	o	$\geqslant -b_2$
y_3		a_{31}	a_{32}	a_{33}	$-a_{34}$	$-a_{35}$	$-a_{36}$	$\geqslant$ o
y_4		a_{41}	a_{42}	a_{43}	$-a_{44}$	$-a_{45}$	$-a_{46}$	$\geqslant$ o
		o	o	o	c_4	c_5	c_6	Max.

TABLE 35

Although Table 35 represents a highly simplified economy in which there are only two types of prime resources, only three productive processes, and three consumption activities, yet it has been kept sufficiently large to encompass in principle two main features of *general* economic analysis (analysis of a complete, or 'closed', system) as contrasted with partial analysis (analysis of an open economy, that is, of part only of the system, as instanced conspicuously in the theory of the firm). These two features are :

(i) Prime resources of more than one kind are used in the economy.

(ii) Any activity (or column of the matrix) may comprise more than one kind of input or more than one kind of output, or, in the case of production activities, more than one kind of input and more than one kind of output. In other words, joint demand for factors, joint supply of products, and joint demand for products are allowed for in the analysis.

'Equilibrium' — that is, equilibrium quantities of inputs and outputs in every activity (or 'industry') ; and equilibrium substitution rates between all inputs and outputs (to which market prices will be equal, if there is a market) — is given by the *solution* of the matrix with its constraints. Thus the values of x's and y's which maximize the subjective value of consumption subject to the given boundary conditions, are the solution.

What characteristics of the economic system (schematized in Table 35) interest us as economists ? What are the features of the system which describe to us the significant differences between one economy and another ? Any economist probably will reply that we are interested in the prices of the system, and in the elasticities. Some people will even put these before the physical quantities — but let us overlook such error of judgment and take it for granted that quantities, produced or consumed, come first on the list. The factor endowment of an economy is certainly one of the most basic things about it. The 'prices' are, more fundamentally, the substitution rates in production and consumption, and the variations in these substitution rates as between different parts of the system displayed in Table 35 incorporate 'elasticities'. When we are asked what features of the economic system interest us, many of us would probably be inclined to stress substitutability — in production, elasticity of supply, and, of course, all the cross elasticities; and in consumption, elasticity of demand, and all the cross elasticities. Clearly in any comparative statics problem much hinges upon the ease with which one activity can be substituted for another, both in production and consumption. It is, of course, quite easy to distinguish an economy with perfect substitutability (constant substitution rates throughout) from one with imperfect substitutability. And at the other extreme we can distinguish economies with no substitutability (rigidly fixed technical coefficients, that is, only one production activity and one consumption activity) from those with several. However, barring these limiting cases substitutability cannot be given any simple meaning. In the general case different parts of the system will show differing substitution rates for each pair of variables, and it will not be possible to characterize the data by reference to any single measure 'substitutability in production' on the one hand, and another measure 'substitutability in consumption' on the other.

Thus, although one may still look out for this feature as an aid in characterizing economies, and tracing the probable effects of changes in data, in rather special cases, we have to recognize that the tool is really of limited application. It will not serve in any but the simplest comparative statics problem. There are, however, other properties of a system of the kind we are using — properties which may be recognized more quickly by a mathematician considering the system as a constrained matrix, than by an economist looking for economic features, but which nevertheless may have economic significance.

The Number of Used Activities does not Exceed the Number of Scarce Commodities

We owe to the mathematical economists[1] a proposition about the equilibrium solution which is by no means obvious from general economic reasoning, and which is of some interest: the solution matrix will be square, or oblong upwards. That is, in order to achieve optimal utilization of resources it will never be necessary to use more activities than there exist effectively scarce commodities of all sorts (inputs and outputs) in the system. It may suffice to use fewer activities than the number of scarce commodities.

Thus if from the matrix giving the complete technological data, with all efficient activities and all physical inputs and outputs listed, we eliminate those columns which represent activities which will not be carried on in the equilibrium position and those rows representing commodities whose value is zero in the equilibrium position, then the remaining matrix of used activities and scarce commodities will have as many columns as it has rows, or else fewer columns. There will not be more activities than scarce commodities.

This proposition was arrived at by mathematical reasoning, and it is perhaps not easy to imbue it with economic significance. The proposition is made not only for the matrix as a whole, but also for the part of it consisting of consumption activities. Here we are told[2] that the number of consumption activities used will be equal to or less than the number of (scarce) goods consumed. The

---

[1] Samuelson, Koopmans and Arrow in *Activity Analysis* (Cowles Commission Monograph 13); R. G. D. Allen, *Mathematical Economics*, chaps. 18 and 19.

[2] See G. B. Dantzig, 'Maximization of a Linear Function of Variables subject to Linear Inequalities', chap. xxi in *Activity Analysis of Production and Allocation* (Ed. Koopmans). Also R. G. D. Allen, *Mathematical Economics*, chaps. 17 and 18.

meaning is, of course, that although there may be a very large number of different commodity-bundles which satisfy the consumer equally, it will always be possible to extract the maximum satisfaction from the total bundle of consumer goods coming out of the production activities, by utilizing only a limited number of consumer-good bundles, namely, as many as there are kinds of consumption goods. This will give full scope for the optimal adaptation of consumption pattern to production pattern. Similarly, on the production side, for any one output the optimal adaptation of production methods to available prime resources can always be attained if as many different technical processes of production are used as there are scarce factors of production. It is not necessary for the entrepreneur to make use of still more (technically available) different production processes in order to adapt to the fullest degree his pattern of production to the pattern of prime resources with which he is endowed.

The Interdependence of Economic Variables

A fundamental property of constrained matrices of the type with which we are dealing is (as we have seen in Chapter V) that they imply simultaneously two sets of equations or inequalities.

On the one hand, there is a set of equations/inequalities obtained from the *row sums*, weighted by the intensities of each activity and equated to (or constrained by) the limits given on the right-hand side of the last column of the matrix. Here the 'weights' or intensities are the unknowns. Their evaluation gives us part of the solution to our economic problem, i.e. it gives us (taken in conjunction with the A-matrix) the equilibrium quantities of all commodities produced and consumed.

On the other hand, there is a set of equations/inequalities obtained from the *column sums*, weighted by the substitution rates of each commodity and equated to (or constrained by) the limits given below the last row of the matrix. The 'weights' are again the unknowns. Their evaluation gives us the other part of the solution of the economic problem, i.e. they give us the (marginal) productivities and (marginal) utilities of all commodities produced and consumed. In an exchange economy these productivities and utilities are equal to the equilibrium market prices. (Note that, if we multiply the productivities and utilities into the corresponding elements of the A-matrix, as we multiply the intensities to get total quantities, we then get total 'outlays' and total 'receipts' evaluated at the equilibrium rates.)

This dual property of the constrained matrix corresponds to the dual solution of the economic problem: the equilibrium quantities and the equilibrium substitution rates (prices) of the economy.

It is familiar to economists that economic variables are mutually interdependent. Nevertheless economic analysts often ignore interdependence, endeavouring to obtain answers to general economic equilibrium problems by the techniques of partial equilibrium analysis. What does the formal consideration of the constrained matrix (Table 35) tell us about interdependence ?

In examining this question we are interested in interdependence between the five sets of variables A b c x and y, that is : technologies ; prime resources ; consumer evaluations ; scales of activity and prices. As economists we are particularly interested in four other sets of variables, namely, the set of quantities of goods consumed ; the value of resources used in each production activity ; the total utility derived from all consumption activities ; and the total cost of all the production activities. These four sets are, of course, implicit in the data A b c x y. The set of goods consumed, say the vector g, is derived by taking the sum of the products of scales of activity in consumption multiplied by the appropriate technical coefficients (in our notation, the sum

$$\sum_{k=q}^{k=v} a_{rk} x_k = g_r (r = e \ldots n),$$

where $k=q$ to $k=v$ denotes those columns which refer to consumption activities and $r=e$ to $r=n$ denotes those rows which refer to consumption goods). The value of resources used in each activity, say the vector h, is derived by taking the sum of the products of prices multiplied by the appropriate technical coefficients in production (in our notation

$$\sum_{r=1}^{r=d} a_{rk} y_r = h_k (k = 1 \ldots p),$$

where $k=1$ to $k=p$ denotes those columns referring to production activities and $r=1$ to $r=d$ denotes those rows referring to factors of production). The total utility obtained from consumption is the sum of the products of utility per unit consumption activity multiplied into the scales of the activities (Σcx). Finally, the total cost of production is the sum of the products of the amount of each prime resource multiplied by its price (Σby). Thus, although our discussion will run in terms of the elementary bricks of our system, the matrix A, the vector b, the vector c, the vector x, and the vector y, these bricks, singly or in simple combination, represent all the familiar economic entities.

In our set of variables the boundary conditions given by resources and tastes (b and c) are 'dual' to each other. Second, the scale or intensity of production and consumption activities, and the substitution rates or prices are 'dual' to each other (x and y are 'dual'). Third, the set of goods of the various kinds consumed is 'dual' to the value of resources used up in the various activities (g 'dual' to h).

Fourth, total utility is dual to total cost (Σcx 'dual' to Σby). The dual variables stand in a special relationship to each other, a proposition in terms of one member of a dual carrying with it the implication of a corresponding (but not always immediately obvious) proposition in terms of its dual.

To simplify our examination of the interdependence of the system, we shall initially exclude variations in the set A other than those which can be transformed into equivalent variations in the sets b and c (see p. 146 below). We shall consider A-variations not thus transformable at a later stage (p. 148 below). We shall here consider primarily the interdependence between b c y x — that is, between resources, tastes, substitution rates (prices) and levels of intensity in each production and consumption activity.

To track down the interdependence more closely, we have set down (Table 36) all the types of variations which can co-exist in a set of four independent vectors and have distinguished therein all those types which, in the interdependent system with which we are dealing, are impossible.

Thus we consider the four vectors b c x y. If these were independent there would be 14 different types of variation, as follows :

> 4 ways of keeping 1 vector only constant
> 6   „   „   2 vectors   „
> 4   „   „   3 vectors   „

The full list of cases is tabulated in Table 36. How many of these can occur in our interdependent economic system ? The answer is not as obvious as might be expected. The following rules may be of help in reaching it. It should be remembered that we are still assuming that technological possibilities in production and consumption (the A-matrix) are constant and unchanged. We are considering what combinations of variations in the vectors b, c, x, y

are possible when we move, in the fashion of comparative statics, from one equilibrium position to another.

I. If neither prime resources (*b* vector) nor final evaluations (*c* vector) vary, no variation in prices (*y* vector) or levels of activities (*x* vector) is possible.[1] Fixing the vectors *c*, *b* fixes the vectors *x*, *y*.

II. Conversely, if neither prices nor levels of activities vary, then *c*, *b* cannot have varied (assuming that the same *b*'s remain scarce before and after the change and apart from variations in factors which are not scarce or evaluations of activities which are not used).

III. If levels of activities do not vary, scarce prime resources cannot have varied (assuming the same *b*'s to be scarce before and after the change).

IV. If prices do not vary, consumer evaluations cannot have varied (assuming that the same consumer activities are used before and after the change and apart from evaluations of unused activities).

These propositions are sufficiently obvious; but their implications are less so. For example, the first one does *not* imply that, if prime resources vary, this by itself makes possible a variation in the equilibrium prices without any other variations. We may therefore note two other rules:

V. A variation in prices other than a strictly proportionate one implies, generally speaking, a variation in activities used (generated by a change either in *b* or in *c*); a strictly proportionate variation in prices may occur with no other change except a proportionate variation in the consumer's final evaluations.

VI. A variation in levels of activities other than a strictly proportionate one (all levels multiplied by a common factor) implies in general a variation in prices (generated by a change either in *b* or in *c*). A strictly proportionate variation in levels of activities may occur with no other

[1] Excluding the possibility of multiple equilibrium.

A.A.—K

change except a proportionate variation in prime resources.

It may be seen (Table 36) that the implications of these six propositions taken together reduce the number of possible combinations of variation and constancy in the four vectors from the 14 that exist for a set of independent vectors, to 4 for our set of interdependent vectors; and of these 4, only 2 permit in general non-proportionate variation. It is possible to vary (disproportionately) quantities of prime resources, levels of activities, and prices, while keeping constant consumers' evaluations. Further, it is possible to vary (disproportionately) consumer evaluations, prices, and levels of activity while keeping constant prime resources. It is also possible to have a *proportionate* variation in each of the vectors prime resources and levels of activities, without any change in prices or final evaluations. Conversely, it is possible to have a proportionate variation in both the price vector and the final evaluations vector, without any change in prime resources or levels of activities. This exhausts the possibilities for our present model. We can never vary one vector in isolation; and no combination of vector variation other than the four referred to above can in general occur either.

In qualification of the above it should be stated that 'variations' in the present context should be understood to mean significant variation: that is, in cases where equilibrium is itself indeterminate over a range variation is understood to mean variation outside that range. Further, our propositions have in several cases been qualified by the words 'generally speaking'. This is because it is often possible to construct special cases to which the proposition does not apply. Our intention is to exclude such special cases; but it should be pointed out that it is not always obvious what constitutes a special case. Indeed our own model is, from a wider point of view, itself a special case.

INTERDEPENDENCE OF PRICES, QUANTITIES OF RESOURCES, ALLOCATION OF RESOURCES, AND CONSUMER EVALUATIONS assuming given technologies in production and consumption.

	Maintain 1 vector / Vary 3 vectors	Maintain 2 vectors / Vary 2 vectors	Maintain 3 vectors / Vary 1 vector
Maintain: c / Vary: bxy	Possible	$\left.\begin{array}{c}cy\\bx\end{array}\right\}$ Possible only in limited cases, by Rule VI	$\left.\begin{array}{c}bxy\\c\end{array}\right\}$
Maintain: b / Vary: cxy	Possible	$\left.\begin{array}{c}bx\\cy\end{array}\right\}$ Possible only in limited cases, by Rule V	$\left.\begin{array}{c}cxy\\b\end{array}\right\}$ All impossible
Maintain: x / Vary: bcy	Impossible by Rule III	$\left.\begin{array}{c}cx\\by\end{array}\right\}$ Impossible by Rule V	$\left.\begin{array}{c}bcy\\x\end{array}\right\}$
Maintain: y / Vary: bcx	Impossible by Rule IV	$\left.\begin{array}{c}by\\cx\end{array}\right\}$ Impossible by Rule VI	$\left.\begin{array}{c}bcx\\y\end{array}\right\}$
Maintain: — / Vary: —		$\left.\begin{array}{c}cb\\xy\end{array}\right\}$ Impossible by Rule I	—
Maintain: — / Vary: —		$\left.\begin{array}{c}xy\\cb\end{array}\right\}$ Impossible by Rule II	—

TABLE 36

Price Elasticities

Let us utilize the above taxonomy to investigate the concept of price elasticity and the related concepts 'income effect' and 'substitution effect'. There cannot be changes in prices and quantities (*y* vector, *x* vector, and the derived vector *ax* for positive *a*-terms, which gives quantity of goods produced in the economy) if there are no changes in either resources or tastes (*b*, *c* vectors; technology is still assumed unchanged). Under a given technology price changes must be generated by variation in prime resources, consumer evaluation, or both. There might be constant tastes (*c*) with varying prices, industry intensities, consumer-good outputs and resources (*y x g b*). Or there might be constant resources, with the other vectors changing. Consider the first case. There is not one but any number of different possible situations. The Partial Equilibrium analyst may instruct us that other things are kept equal; the only thing we know about this problem is that other things cannot be kept equal. The change in *g* and *y* is, in this case, caused by a change in the vector *b*. It does not seem that the instruction 'keep other things equal' can provide any basis for determining the accompanying changes in *g*, *y*, and also *x*.

In general, however, we may not even know whether the price-quantity change which we wish to study is generated by a change in the vector *b* or in the vector *c*. Thus to give to the concept 'Price Elasticity' (or the corresponding concept in absolute terms, 'Price Effect') any definite meaning, we have to specify in full the variation in the *b* and/or *c* vectors which generates the price-quantity change. There are as many different 'price elasticities' as there are combinations of such *b/c* variations.

Let us consider further the analysis of price-quantity changes. Taking the variation in absolute (not relative) terms, Slutzky's equation, referring to a partial economy under infinitesimal variations, splits the 'price effect' into two conceptually distinct parts: the Income Effect and the Substitution Effect.[1] The substitution effect is defined as the change in the quantity of any given commodity that would be consumed if income changed in such a way as to make it just possible (but not optimal) for the consumer to buy at the new equilibrium prices the same bundle of commodities as he bought before the price change.

The difficulty in this definition lies in the difficulty of defining, not the position to which the consumer goes finally (if the data change giving rise to the price change is fully specified, this can be done) but the conceptual interim position from which we measure the said change. This conceptual interim position which establishes both the income effect and also the substitution effect (the point S in Mosak's diagram in his article in *Mathematical Studies in Economics and Econometrics*) is defined, for infinitesimal changes in a partial system, in the Slutzky equation. In our system, which is complete or closed and which undergoes finite changes, we shall define the interim position by the vector ax which would obtain in equilibrium if the y vector were as in the final equilibrium position, but the 'income' of the consumer were so deflated (or inflated) that the initial x vector would yield an *efficient* collection of goods (i.e. the old quantities could still be obtained, and only just obtained, with the new resources), but this would not be the optimal collection. That is, the preferred position of the consumer would, at the new prices with the deflated income, yield a vector x different from either the initial vector or the final vector.

Is such an interim position unique? In other words, has the required 'income deflation' (inflation) only one value? In partial equilibrium analysis uniqueness is obtained, of course, by the identification of 'income' with

[1] J. R. Hicks, *Value and Capital*, Mathematical Appendix, § 7.

a single good : Money. In general equilibrium analysis the 'income deflation' represents a manipulation of the b vector. With discrete production activities it may be shown that there is, in general, no unique income deflation and hence no unique income effect and no unique substitution effect.

The above points may be illustrated numerically by the following tables.

	ACTIVITIES						RESOURCES (b)
	PRODUCTION			CONSUMPTION			
	I	II	III	IV	V	VI	
Intensities (x)	o	1	1	1·87	2·38	o	
Prices (y)							
1·35	− 12	− 10	− 8	o	o	o	⩾ − 18
1·30	− 3	− 5	− 9	o	o	o	⩾ − 14
2·50	2	4	7	− 3·33	− 2	− 1·11	⩾ o
5·00	3	2	1	− 0·33	− 1	− 1·67	⩾ o
Utilities (c)	o	o	o	10	10	10	Max.

Quantity of first Output = 11
„ second „ = 3
Total utility = 42·5

TABLE 37

	ACTIVITIES						RESOURCES (b)
	PRODUCTION			CONSUMPTION			
	I	II	III	IV	V	VI	
Intensities (x)	2	1	o	o	2	3·6	
Prices (y)							
1	− 12	− 10	− 8	o	o	o	⩾ − 34
2	− 3	− 5	− 9	o	o	o	⩾ − 11
3	2	4	7	− 3·33	− 2	− 1·11	⩾ o
4	3	2	1	− 0·33	− 1	− 1·67	⩾ o
Utilities (c)	o	o	o	10	10	10	Max.

Quantity of first Output = 8
„ second „ = 8
Total utility = 56

TABLE 38

	ACTIVITIES						RESOURCES
	PRODUCTION			CONSUMPTION			(b)
	I	II	III	IV	V	VI	
tensities (x)	1·5	1·5	0	0	3	2·7	
ces (y)							
1	− 12	− 10	− 8	0	0	0	⩾ − 33
2	− 3	− 5	− 9	0	0	0	⩾ − 12
3	2	4	7	− 3·33	− 2	− 1·11	⩾ 0
4	3	2	1	− 0·33	− 1	− 1·67	⩾ 0
ilities (c)	0	0	0	10	10	10	Max.

Quantity of first Output = 9
,, second ,, = 7·5
Total utility = 57

TABLE 39

	ACTIVITIES							RESOURCES
	PRODUCTION				CONSUMPTION			(b)
	I	II	III	III*a*	IV	V	VI	
tensities (x)	2·5	0·3	0	0	0	0·6	4·5	
ices (y)								
1	− 12	− 10	− 8	− 16·5	0	0	0	⩾ − 33
2	− 3	− 5	− 9	− 4·5	0	0	0	⩾ − 9
3	2	4	7	5·5	− 3·33	− 2	− 1·11	⩾ 0
4	3	2	1	1·5	− 0·33	− 1	− 1·67	⩾ 0
tilities (c)	0	0	0	0	10	10	10	Max.

Quantity of first Output = 6·2
,, second ,, = 8·1
Total utility = 51

TABLE 40

	ACTIVITIES							RESOURCE
	PRODUCTION				CONSUMPTION			(b)
	I	II	III	III*a*	IV	V	VI	
Intensities (x)	0·42	2·05	0	0	0	4·10	0·75	
Prices (y)								
1	−12	−10	−8	−16·5	0	0	0	⩾ −25·5
2	−3	−5	−9	−4·5	0	0	0	⩾ −11·5
3	2	4	7	5·5	−3·33	−2	−1·11	⩾ 0
4	3	2	1	1·5	−0·33	−1	−1·67	⩾ 0
Utilities (c)	0	0	0	0	10	10	10	Max.

Quantity of first Output = 9·03
,, second ,, = 5·35
Total utility = 48·5

TABLE 41

Table 37 shows initial data (A *b c*) and equilibrium
solution (*x*, *y*, implying *g*). Table 38 gives the new
equilibrium solution (*x* y** implying *g**) resulting from a
given change in data (*b* changes to *b**). Table 39 shows
that if we had chosen a different change in data (*b* changes
to *b***) the *given* price change is associated with a different
change in the quantity vector, that is, with discrete production activities our price effect is indeterminate unless
we specify the change in data which generates it. Tables
40 and 41 show that, even given the causal change in data
(from *b* to *b**) as shown in Tables 37 and 38, the 'income
effect' and 'substitution effect' within the 'price effect'
still remain undefined because there is no basis (even with
complete knowledge of all facts) for defining the 'income
compensation'. Tables 40 and 41 are based on two
different arbitrary income compensations, as indicated on
p. 135 above, and give two different measures of income
and substitution effects. The extra production activity
III*a* is inserted to show that we have conformed to the
condition that in the interim position the old collection of

goods should be efficient but not optimal. In Table 40 Activity III*a* could be used to produce the old collection without waste of physical resources, but under it cost exceeds value : in Table 41 Activity III*a* could be used with II and III to produce the old collection without waste of resources, but again cost would exceed value. This activity III*a* should be envisaged as being also available in the matrices of Tables 37, 38, and 39 ; but since in all the conditions considered the cost of the inputs exceeds that of the outputs, it would not be used anywhere. This is as it should be.

Assume now that data change as from Table 37 to Table 38. If we adopt Table 40 as the basis of the interim position, the income effect upon Output I is to change the quantity consumed from 6·2 to 8 ; the other part of the change (namely from 11 to 6·2) being ascribed to substitution effect. If we adopt Table 41 as the basis of the interim position, we should say that the income effect changes the quantity from 9·03 to 8, and the substitution effect from 11 to 9·03.

Monetary Analysis and Analysis in Real Terms

The rigid explicit model with which we are working serves to reveal certain pitfalls encountered in economic analysis carried out in monetary terms.

The term 'money' is used to mean many different things. With our highly formalized representation of the economic system the different meanings become sharply distinguished. There are three logical possibilities : either 'money' is the only scarce commodity (such an approximation may be appropriate and is often used in analysis of the firm — i.e. partial equilibrium) ; or it is one of several scarce commodities ; or it is purely a *numéraire*. In the last case prices of all goods are enumerated in terms of their rate of substitution (value) against some one good. Inspection of the matrix (Table 35) will show that the *numéraire* good may be any prime resource or consumer good, or it may also be any bundle of consumer goods yielding a certain psychological 'good' to the consumer, i.e. one of the *c*'s.   In the form in which we have been using the matrix the *c*'s have been normalized (as may always be done for *one* of the vectors *b*, *c*, *y* by suitable choice of units) so that they are all equal, and we have been treating the (constant) amount of utility derived by the various consumption bundles as our unit of measurement of values, that is, as the *numéraire*.

The interpretation of 'money' as a *numéraire* only is the most general treatment.   Cases where the *numéraire* is at the same time the only scarce good, or one of a number of scarce producer and consumer goods, appear as special cases of the general case.

Our formulation enables us to see the implications of the treatment of money as a 'veil' merely covering but not altering the real features of the economy, and to contrast this with the treatment of money as a factor influencing the real features.   For this purpose we assume that the economy is undergoing some change or changes, which we analyse by the method of comparative statics.

Now, of all the combinations of vector changes only one conforms to the monetary veil interpretation, namely, a proportionate change in all prices (*y*).   In no other case do 'monetary changes' leave real factors strictly unchanged.

If money is treated not as a *numéraire* but as a scarce resource, it can clearly not be treated as a veil.   If it is the only scarce resource, then variations in the quantity of money produce no change in prices of resources or consumer goods, but a proportionate change in all physical quantities.   This is the case referred to at the top of the second column of Table 36, where a proportionate variation in the vectors *b*, *x* is listed as consistent with constant prices and consumer evaluations.

While these two cases, of proportionate changes in prices with no change in real quantities, and proportionate changes in quantities with no change in prices respectively, are opposite to each other in a sense, they are similar to each other in an important respect: *analysis in money terms* will give a correct answer in both cases. This is simply because with constant relative prices evaluation in terms of any single *numéraire* reflects precisely not merely 'money values' but at the same time the real values. If, for instance, the utility derived from all forms of consumption (c vector) increases by $\frac{1}{10}$, then the monetary evaluation (Σcx) goes up by the same proportion, in conformity with the real situation.

The two cases of proportionate changes in all resources (and activity levels) with no valuation changes on the one hand, and proportionate changes in all valuations with no physical quantity changes on the other, are, however, highly special. Suppose, for instance, that money is one among several scarce factors (buildings, plant, transport) then an increase in the quantity of money only will not lead to a proportionate increase in output; it will, in general, cause a change in relative prices of the system. As soon as this happens, monetary analysis ceases to be a precise tool. It becomes an approximation, which amounts to evaluating diverse changes in physical quantities of a heterogeneous collection of goods by applying the previous (now inaccurate) relative values. It will occur to the reader that there is a dual procedure which might be followed: to evaluate diverse changes in the prices of a heterogeneous collection of goods by applying previous (now inaccurate) relative quantities.

In other words, to the widespread practice of ignoring changes in relative prices in order to get a unique comparative evaluation of two positions there exists a symmetrical possibility: to ignore changes in relative quantities. Where relative quantities are somewhat rigid and price fluctuations violent, the latter procedure is likely to be less inaccurate than the former.   The only type of case in which variations in quantities consumed give a completely accurate measure of variations in utility (assuming that the relevant utility function, for individual or group, can be formulated) is where relative prices *and relative quantities* are unchanged. In this case a measure of gain (loss) based on the assumption of constant proportions between goods consumed is completely accurate : and so also is a measure based on the assumption of constant relative prices.   As soon as relative prices are not constant and an approximation or index number is sought, it is an open question whether the closest approximation is given by valuing bundles of goods of changing composition at constant prices (initial prices or final prices or some average of these two) ; or by reckoning the amount of a bundle of goods of *un*changing composition that can be obtained.   But as soon as we exclude the limiting case and deal with the general case of varying proportions and prices, it is no longer a matter of indifference which index we use.

An example of a case where the assumption of constant prices would even indicate the wrong direction of change in total utility, while the assumption of constant relative quantities would give the correct direction and a reasonable approximation, is as follows.   Let the original data be as follows :

	ACTIVITIES					RESOURCES
	I	II	III	IV	V	
	-1	-4	0	0	0	$\geqslant -50$
	-7	-1	0	0	0	$\geqslant -80$
	12	8	-25	-10	-9	$\geqslant 0$
	8	12	-8	-10	-11	$\geqslant 0$
Utility	0	0	20	20	20	Max.

TABLE 42

Equilibrium Intensities $x_1 = 10$; $x_2 = 10$; $x_3 = 0$; $x_4 = 20$; $x_5 = 0$.

Equilibrium Prices $y_1 = \dfrac{120}{27}$; $y_2 = \dfrac{60}{27}$; $y_3 = 1$; $y_4 = 1$.

Utility $= 20\ x_4 = 400$.

Let resources change from $\left.\begin{array}{l}50\\80\end{array}\right\}$ to $\left.\begin{array}{l}44\frac{1}{2}\\95\frac{1}{2}\end{array}\right\}$ all other data remaining unchanged. Then the new equilibrium is:

Intensities $x_1 = 12\frac{1}{2}$; $x_2 = 8$; $x_3 = \dfrac{18}{17}$; $x_4 = \dfrac{3188}{170}$; $x_5 = 0$.

Prices $y_1 = \dfrac{2456}{459}$; $y_2 = \dfrac{760}{459}$; $y_3 = \dfrac{4}{17}$; $y_4 = \dfrac{30}{17}$.

Utility $= 20\ x_3 + 20\ x_4 = 396\frac{4}{17}$

Thus we have:

	Originally	In New Situation
Correct Measure of Utility	400	$396\frac{4}{17}$
Utility measured by taking the new quantities and valuing at the old relative prices		410
Utility measured by taking the old relative quantities (and limiting absolute quantities by the new output of the effectively scarce commodity, which is 196)		$\dfrac{196}{200} \times 400 = 392$

We have to remember that, in general, knowledge of consumer-good prices and quantities (vectors x, y) is insufficient to tell us what is happening to total utility (Σcx). Consideration of the effect of a certain change in the tariff system (tax system) upon the volume of international trade (domestic trade) cannot tell us what is happening to community welfare (even assuming that we know how to add individuals' utilities). Similarly, knowledge of variations in quantities and prices of prime resources is insufficient for deriving variations in the outlays in the different production processes.

To sum up, it emerges from the above that the comparative statics problems with which economists are most concerned involve the simultaneous variation of more than one vector, and in many cases all vectors will be varying : resources, tastes, allocation of resources to each industry, prices and consumer-good quantities. Those seeking to tackle economic analysis by means of partial equilibrium techniques have been aware of this. They have chosen to ignore some of the interactions of the system in order to reduce the problem to manageable proportions. But it seems that such a simplification, while in itself often desirable, is not acceptable if it is made blindly, without prior consideration of the magnitude of the elements excluded and included in the analysis. Thus in the above example of estimating changes in utility from changes in quantity consumed, it may sometimes be justifiable to avoid solving the full system of interdependent equations (inequalities) and to construct instead some rough index number procedure. But, if so, it is essential to consider *in principle* the whole system so as to construct an informative index number, based on a significant selection of the elements to be included in the analysis.

The Direction of Large Changes and the Direction of Small Changes

The last property of the system to which we draw attention is this : given the economic system as traditionally interpreted it is not necessarily true that the direction of change — say in total utility — shown by a very small variation in data will be the same as the direction of change for a larger (discrete) variation in the data. The fact that the first derivative of the utility function with respect to a given variable is positive at a given point is no guarantee that, for finite changes, utility will be increased by increasing that variable. We may be in the neighbourhood of a local maximum merely. If in a walk through the countryside we seek to reach the highest point in a given area, the fact that at the spot where we are standing the ground is rising to the north is no guarantee that the highest peak lies in that direction; we may be standing on the slopes of a small local eminence, with the peak to the south of us.

An economic problem which is equivalent to a constrained matrix is correctly solved by solving the system of simultaneous equations/inequalities given by the matrix. If we 'break down' the problem and substitute 'step-by-step' procedures this always gives a correct solution if at each step we take into account either all the rows of selected columns, or all the columns of selected rows.[1] By contrast a step-by-step procedure which considers successively partial systems consisting of sub-matrices, need not necessarily give the solution of the whole system. Economic models equivalent to this latter procedure cannot be relied upon for correct solutions.

Variations in the A-matrix: the Distinction between Variations in Technology and Variations in Efficiency

Hitherto we have considered only two types of variations in data: variations in the b vector (signifying changes in prime resources) and variations in the c vector (signifying changes in tastes). Formally, we can clearly also vary the A-matrix itself. Before considering the economic meaning of such variation, let us note a point that occurs to one from a purely formal consideration of the matrix: any change in the A-matrix which amounts to a proportionate change in all the elements of any row (or rows) is equivalent to a change in the corresponding element (or elements) of the b vector, in the sense that either formulation gives the

[1] I am indebted to Dr. Morton for this point.

same solution for prices and levels of activity. Any change in the A-matrix which amounts to a proportionate change in all the elements of any column (or columns) is equivalent to a proportionate change in the corresponding element (or elements) of the c vector, in the sense that either formulation gives the same solution for prices and levels of activity. Any change in the A-matrix which represents a combination of such proportionate variations can be depicted by a combination of changes in the b and c vectors. For example, suppose that initially we had the following matrix:

	ACTIVITIES			RESOURCES	
I	II	III	IV		
-6	-9	o	o	$\geqslant -15$	
-14	-6	o	o	$\geqslant -20$	
3	8	-2	$-2\frac{1}{2}$	$\geqslant$ o	
10	2	-16	-1	$\geqslant$ o	
o	o	1	1	Max.	

TABLE 43

Suppose next that this matrix changed in the following way :

All the figures in row 1 of the body of the matrix are divided by 3.

All the figures in row 2 of the body of the matrix are divided by 2.

All the figures in column 3 of the body of the matrix are divided by 2.

All the figures in column 4 of the body of the matrix are multiplied by 4.

We can use for our new constrained matrix either a matrix (Table 44) where these divisions and multiplications have been carried out on all the elements inside the matrix ; or, alternatively, we can use a matrix (Table 45) with the old a-elements and appropriately altered b and c boundaries.

	ACTIVITIES				RESOURCES
	I	II	III	IV	
Intensities	1	4·33	0·47	3·72	
Prices (approx.)					
$y_1 = \cdot 04$	−2	−3	0	0	⩾ −15
$y_2 = \cdot 18$	−7	−3	0	0	⩾ −20
$y_3 = \cdot 05$	3	8	−1	−10	⩾ 0
$y_4 = \cdot 12$	10	2	−8	−4	⩾ 0
	0	0	1	1	Max.

TABLE 44

	ACTIVITIES				RESOURCES
	I	II	III	IV	
Intensities	1	4·33	0·24	14·88	
Prices (approx.)					
$y_1 = \cdot 013$	−6	−9	0	0	⩾ −45
$y_2 = \cdot 09$	−14	−6	0	0	⩾ −40
$y_3 = \cdot 05$	3	8	−2	−2·5	⩾ 0
$y_4 = \cdot 12$	10	2	−16	−1	⩾ 0
	0	0	2	·25	Max.

TABLE 45

The solution in terms of intensities of activities in each industry (x), total goods produced (g), and prices (y), *when expressed in the same units as previously*, is the same which-ever matrix is used. All we have really done is to re-quote our production coefficients and our consumption activities in different units. Thus in Table 45 the price for the second input, for instance, refers to the price of, say, half a man-hour instead of one man-hour. And the price for this amount of this commodity will read half as high as when we use Table 44. In other words, the price is the same under both methods of computation. Similarly for the first input. On the consumption side it is the unit level of activity which has been changed; hence the

A.A.—L

computed intensities must be changed in inverse proportion in order to leave the real answer unchanged. For instance, Consumption Activity III is carried on at level 0·47 if the unit level is as defined in Table 44; it is carried on at half that level if the unit level is doubled as in Table 45.

Are, then, all possible changes in data comprised in changes in the b vector and the c vector (in prime resources and tastes)? From our economic knowledge we know that this is not so, because there may be changes in known technology. Mathematically, we also know that it is not so, because while all changes in b and c can be represented by (proportionate) changes in the rows and columns of the A-matrix, the converse is not true. In other words, even though we may alter all the b's and all the c's, each single change necessarily produces a *proportionate* change in the row (or column) of a's; and however many such proportionate variations we superimpose upon each other we shall not be able to arrive at all possible new a-sets. For example, if the A-matrix changes from $\begin{pmatrix} 1 & 2 \\ 4 & 1 \end{pmatrix}$ to $\begin{pmatrix} 1 & 8 \\ 12 & 6 \end{pmatrix}$ it is not possible to represent this change by any combination of changes in b and c.

A factor of production may be defined by reference to what it will do, to its 'efficiency'. Thus, suppose that new knowledge or efficiency renders it possible to carry on all activities (with given outputs and given inputs for all commodities but the first) using only half as much of the first input. This could be depicted by halving the a-elements in the first row, or alternatively by doubling the b boundary in the first row. When we do the latter we are in effect defining this factor in efficiency, rather than in any physical or quasi-physical, terms. Suppose, for instance, the factor is labour, and we have initially 100 man-hours, as boundary to a given A-matrix. The reduction of all labour-inputs to one-half of their initial value may equally well be expressed as a doubling of the available quantity of man-hours of the *old* efficiency. Thus we define Labour (and similarly all other inputs) in terms of its efficiency. The same is true, *mutatis mutandis*, of changes in a-columns bounded by c's.

Thus proportionate changes in rows and/or columns, which can be depicted by changes in the b and/or c vectors, may be interpreted as changes in efficiency of factors of production and/or the utility of consumer-good bundles. This being so, such changes may be incorporated in the model by expressing each b and c in terms of a *standard* efficiency, i.e. adjusting the numerical value of the b's and c's whenever their efficiency changes. Such a procedure is, of course, familiar to economists : we often try to adjust figures for man-hours of labour of different qualities to a figure of an equivalent number of man-hours of homogeneous labour units.

Technological changes may then be defined as such changes in the A-matrix (the 'production coefficients' and the corresponding 'consumption coefficients') as cannot be translated into equivalent changes in efficiency of factors and outputs. To confine the term 'technological change' so as to exclude overall changes in the efficiency of goods is, of course, a matter of terminology. But it is useful to distinguish, by whatever terms, alterations in data which can be reduced to general changes in the efficiency of a factor (factors) or output (outputs) applied in given technical processes, from alterations in data which change the inter-relationships of the technical processes themselves. The latter type of change is more radical. It breaks up the internal structure of the production (consumption) function, so that we can no longer identify technical processes (whether used or not used in the equilibrium position) in the new situation, with technical processes in the old situation : nor can we define factors or products in units which are homogeneous for the two situations.

We conclude that, so far as concerns our study of the interdependence of the economic variables, changes in the A-matrix may be of a kind which is equivalent to changes in the vectors *b* and *c*, the implications of which upon the system of interdependent variables we have already examined. Alternatively, changes in the A-matrix may be of the kind we have defined as 'technological', in which case the break in data is so radical as to make further analysis of the variations in the whole system of variables appear unprofitable.

The Special Case or the General Case?

One of the disadvantages of handling our analysis by means of simple tables, numerical examples, and geo-metrical diagrams, instead of mathematically, is that it is not always clear how general or how special are the cases we are handling and the solutions we are giving. This question is one which has to be continually borne in mind in reading this book. It is not possible to give a general answer to it. But we shall try in the remaining paragraphs of this chapter to give some indication of the respects in which, in terms of our model, certain forms of analysis — and among them our own — may be regarded as special cases.

First, even within the limits of the basic postulates underlying our analysis, a formulation of the type we have been using (for instance, in Table 32) can be made into a special case by the selection of actual numerical values for the A-matrix and the vectors *b*, *c*. Slightly less crude than this, we can also bias our case by the selection of the ratios of these values. One particular way of selecting values is to put certain things equal to zero. The differences between many economic models may be accounted for by differences in the selection of variables which are equated to zero.

Degenerate Systems

The formalization of the economic system adopted in Table 32 suggests that different types of simplification will be introduced into the model by putting zeros in various parts of the matrix and its boundaries, in such a way as to reduce certain vectors to single variables. The significantly different ways in which this can be done in our model are as follows:

Simplification 1: we might reduce the vector of inputs (negative coefficients) in any productive activity to a single coefficient.

Simplification 2: we might reduce the vector of outputs (positive coefficients) in any productive activity to a single coefficient.

Simplification 3: we might reduce the vector of boundaries for prime resources to a single coefficient.

Simplification 4: we might reduce the vector of inputs (negative coefficients) in any consumer activity to a single coefficient.

Simplification 5: we might reduce the vector of boundaries for final utility to a single coefficient.

These cases are indicated for a six by six matrix in Table 46.

Simplifications 1, 2, and 4 are commonly adopted in the exposition of marginal productivity and marginal utility theory. By excluding simultaneous jointness in both inputs and outputs, theorists are able to abstract from production processes and the substitution of such processes for each other, and adhere to simple definitions of marginal

This figure cannot be rendered as a data table because each "cell" is a circle-type marker (solid, dashed, or concentric). Transcribing per the matrix rules, every marker is preserved in its row/column position. The five grids each have an ACTIVITIES header spanning Production and Consumption columns, and COMMODITIES as the row label.

Simplification 1
ACTIVITIES — Production | Consumption

	P1	P2	P3	C1	C2	C3	
1		○	○	◌	◌	◌	
2	○		○	◌	◌	◌	
3	○	○		◌	◌	◌	
4							◌
5							◌
6							◌
	◎	◎	◎				

Simplification 2
ACTIVITIES — Production | Consumption

	P1	P2	P3	C1	C2	C3	
1				◌	◌	◌	
2				◌	◌	◌	
3				◌	◌	◌	
4		○	○				◎
5	○		○				◎
6	○	○					◎
	◎	◎	◎				

Simplification 3
ACTIVITIES — Production | Consumption

	P1	P2	P3	C1	C2	C3	
1				◌	◌	◌	
2	○	○	○	◌	◌	◌	○
3	○	○	○	◌	◌	◌	○
4							◌
5							◌
6							◌
	◌	◌	◌				

Simplification 4
ACTIVITIES — Production | Consumption

	P1	P2	P3	C1	C2	C3	
1				◎	◎	◎	
2				◎	◎	◎	
3				◎	◎	◎	
4					○	○	◌
5				○		○	◌
6				○	○		◌
	◌	◌	◌				

Simplification 5
ACTIVITIES — Production | Consumption

	P1	P2	P3	C1	C2	C3	
1				◌	◎	◎	
2				◌	◎	◎	
3				◌	◎	◎	
4					○	○	◌
5					○	○	◌
6					○	○	◌
	◌	◌	◌		○	○	

Legend:

◌ indicates made zero in the present analysis

○ indicates made zero in other analysis

◎ indicates made zero in the present and in other analysis

TABLE 46

products and rates of substitution between factors. The various substitution rates of the system are illustrated in the text-books as the slopes of isoquants, production possibility curves, and indifference curves; but the forms ascribed to these curves (the changes in the substitution rates) are asserted rather than explained.

The simplification of assuming only one type of prime resource (which implies also absence of joint inputs) characterizes economic analysis in monetary terms. When particular equilibrium is discussed (whether it is a firm producing for profit or a consumer shopping for satisfaction) it has been customary to present the analysis in monetary terms. Within such a framework it is possible to analyse (changes in) quantities and relative prices of the commodities of the system — that is, of the various consumer goods (and intermediate goods). It is not possible to analyse levels of activity in different productive processes, i.e. the allocation of productive resources, or relative prices of prime resources. This limitation includes within it the limitation that monetary analysis cannot instruct us on problems involving changes in idle and bottleneck (limitational) factors of production (changes in the set of factors with positive values).

The analysis of the equilibrium of the firm is rendered incomplete when the diversity of resources is neglected. In order to get a finite solution at all 'decreasing returns' must be introduced somewhere. Rigorous pursuit of the source of these will lead us back to the existence of more than one boundary condition.[1] Analogous short-

---

[1] An example of an erroneous theoretical conclusion arising from a monetary approach to the theory of the firm is the idea that factors of production cannot be 'inferior'. In fact, convexity of the production function does not preclude the possibility that a change in data may bring about a fall in the price of a factor associated with a fall in the quantity of it which is bought. See H. Makower and William J. Baumol, 'The Analogy between Producer and Consumer Equilibrium Analysis', *Economica*, February 1950. Also J. M. Naharro Mora, 'Las analogías entre la producción y el consumo', *Moneda y Credito*, December 1949.

comings enter into monetary treatment of consumer behaviour in the market, as has already been indicated above.

More serious difficulties arise when analysis of broader fields of the economy is treated in monetary terms. One such field is international trade. The *raison d'être* of international trade lies in differing prime resources and/or differing consumer tastes, in different countries. The latter element, though logically it could on its own create all the profit from trade, in practice does not appear to be mainly responsible for this profit (inasmuch as the principal exports of most countries are usually staple items of consumption in the producing country) and is anyhow not easy to analyse further in economic terms. Most of our analysis of international trade — of the gain to be derived from it, or the loss to be suffered by restricting it in various ways — rests on international differences in costs of production, and these rest on international differences in prime resources. In other words, problems concerning gains or losses accompanying various systems of facilitation or restriction of international trade are problems of allocation of resources between different productive activities, and require explicit treatment of more than one type of real resource. It is, of course, obvious that analysis based on a single prime resource cuts out consideration not only of varying relative quantities of (prime) factors of production but also of varying prices of these factors. Yet it seems to have taken a century to appreciate the full implications of this fact in the field of international trade theory. The Labour Theory of Value was, in effect, like a monetary model of resources combined with a single kind of consumption activity (Simplifications 3 and 5). The sole type of prime resource was Labour. From such a model it is not possible to deduce either factor prices or allocation of resources. All published attempts to do so prior to 1948 appear to have failed.[1] Professors Samuelson [2] and Lerner [3] solve the problem by treating — explicitly — two prime resources instead of one. Quite similarly comparative statics problems of a single country may often arise from non-proportionate changes in the set of real resources, and these cannot be elucidated in terms of a single prime resource. One example of such problems is a long-term change in the balance between labour, capital, and land in the community. Another example (arising in dynamic systems) is a short-term change in the balance between specific capital equipment used in particular industries and other factors of production. Such changes often imply not only changes in the relative quantities of available prime resources, but also changes in the set of effectively limitational (or scarce) factors of production. Problems of unemployment and unused capacity can only be satisfactorily analysed in monetary terms alone if, and in so far as, the unemployment of labour, machinery, and all other important factors, is quite general throughout the system.[4]

The Simplifications 4 and 5 are 'dual' to Simplifications 1 and 3. Both of them concern consumer activities. Simplification 5 means that all consumer goods are rigidly complementary, the consumption pattern being fixed. It comprises within it Simplification 4, i.e. that any consumption activity contains only one type of consumer good (for although under 5 we still have three physical goods entering

---

[1] For instance, Haberler's treatment (*Theory of International Trade*) does not solve the problem. The 'opportunity costs' are still only in terms of output substitution rates, the input substitution rates (factor prices) remaining buried.

[2] 'International Trade and the Equalization of Factor Prices' *Economic Journal*, June 1948 ; 'International Factor-Price Equalization Once Again', *Economic Journal*, June 1949.

[3] 'Factor Prices and International Trade', *Economica*, February 1952.

[4] That it was thus general in the Great Depression is the assumption underlying Keynes' *General Theory of Employment, Interest and Money*. Hayek's trade cycle analysis goes out from very different assumptions in this respect.

into consumption, they are rigidly complementary and can be treated as a single economic good). Simplification 4 does not, however, imply 5, for under 4 there is more than one consumer activity. Simplification 4, although less drastic than 5, is patently unrepresentative of consumer tastes in general, for it implies that the utility derived from all the different goods is entirely independent (additive preference function).

In looking round for the 'dual' to Simplification 2 — if not before — the reader will have noticed three other simplifications which we ourselves have made in nearly all of our models. We have put zeros for the row boundaries for consumer goods; we have put zeros for the column boundaries for production activities, and we have put zeros for the prime factor coefficients in the consumer activities. The last simplification precludes dual-purpose goods, i.e. goods used both for producing other goods and for direct consumption (such as, e.g., coal). In other words, we assume that no goods used for final consumption are prime factors of production. Various other simplifications might be made. One could, for instance, set up the model where all goods used for final consumption are prime factors which would either give only consumption activities or — if 'produced factors of production' are included — it would give a matrix with entries in production activities for both prime and produced factors, but entries in consumption activities for prime factors only, i.e. zeros throughout the bottom right-hand quadrant. This would not, however, be of much interest. The simplifications we have used are less unreal. Nevertheless for some problems the omission of commodities such as coal which are important both as factors of production and as consumption goods is unwarranted. For such problems a model with entries in the top right-hand quadrant of the matrix should be used.

Our assumption that the row boundaries for consumer goods are zero implies that there is no production which is not for consumption. We have ourselves removed this restriction in considering production for taxes (Chapter VIII). In a dynamic model where production for stock may be important, one might depict this by inserting positive lower limits for the excess of output of consumer goods over consumption of them. In other words, for any analysis going beyond the static limits we have laid down for ourselves here, the model would not assume these boundaries to be zero.

The assumption of zero utilities from production activities is also restricting. For certain problems it may be desirable to generalize this assumption to allow of positive utilities from production.

All of the different simplifications discussed above — both those we have ourselves used and those we have not — are special cases of the general case. The validity or otherwise of working with special cases depends upon the context in which they are used and the significance which is attached to the conclusions based upon them. In judging the analysis presented in this book the reader is reminded once more that the treatment lacks generality not only in respect of the variables assumed to be zero, but also through the use of actual values (where such are used) for the variables. On the other hand, special cases may serve to disprove a general proposition.

CHAPTER XI

AN APPLICATION OF ACTIVITY ANALYSIS TO A PROBLEM IN COMPARATIVE STATICS

The Ricardo Effect

Is it possible that an increase in the price of consumption goods can cause a fall in the relative profitability of longer processes of production as compared with shorter processes, and hence a reduction in the demand for capital goods? And is it possible that a fall in the rate of interest can cause a shift to more *labour*-intensive methods of production? Extensive discussion of these and related questions may be found in the works of Professor Hayek.[1] The first of the above reactions, namely, that a rise in consumer good prices may cause a shift to shorter processes of production and a reduction in the demand for capital goods, is defined by Professor Hayek as 'the Ricardo Effect'.[2] His analysis of this is carried out first of all under the abstraction of an economy in which there is no lending of money of any kind. In fact, the model of this part of the analysis can be constructed entirely in terms of physical goods. Later on Professor Hayek re-introduces money and credit, and proceeds to consider 'the central issue': effects of changes in the rate of interest in conjunction with changes in prices of goods. This implies a

---

[1] 'The Ricardo Effect', *Economica*, May 1942; reprinted in *Individualism and Economic Order. The Pure Theory of Capital*, chaps. xxi and xxvii.

[2] *Individualism and Economic Order*, p. 223. See also p. 234.

much more complex system. As Professor Hayek says,[1] 'To take account of the complicated relations of technological (and psychological) complementarity which are involved requires another technique. . . . Here all that we shall mention is that if we were to start from a complete statement of the substitution relationships between all the different resources concerned, all kinds of peculiarities and apparent anomalies in the behaviour of individual factors would appear to be quite consistent with the general tendencies which can be deduced from the cruder type of analysis. It is, for instance, quite possible that while a fall in the rate of interest will create a tendency for the services of most of the permanent factors to be invested for longer periods and for their prices to rise, in the case of some individual factor the effect may well be that it will be invested for shorter periods, or that its price will be lowered, or both.' We shall give one or two examples of such 'apparent anomalies' in particular cases. The technique of activity analysis gives us the required 'complete statement of the substitution relationships between the different resources concerned'. If we construct very simple cases we can handle all of the relevant inter-relationships. In what follows below, after considering the Ricardo Effect in an economy without borrowing, we shall construct a model with money and give one or two examples of the 'apparent anomalies' that can arise with changes in interest rates.

A Single-Factor Firm in a World of Barter

Professor Hayek has defined the 'Ricardo Effect' in an economy without credit as follows : a fall in wages relative to product prices will increase the profitability of less capital-intensive methods more than it increases the

[1] *Pure Theory of Capital*, pp. 291-2.

profitability of more capital-intensive methods.[1]   In our simple model methods employing relatively less capital must be taken to be the short method, those employing relatively more capital the long method.   Professor Hayek's proposition means then that an increase in output prices relative to wages, everything else remaining constant, will cause the entrepreneur to shift to the shorter process.   Is this true ?

Table 47 depicts a firm owning initially certain goods, and unable to borrow.   These goods are the final product of the economy and constitute at once the wage-good of labour and the profit of the entrepreneur.   They are all of one kind (or they may be a bundle of things used together in fixed proportions throughout the exercise).   We have called them in the table 'loaves'.   The entrepreneur has at his disposal 100 of these.   There is a single productive factor, say labour, which can be purchased on the market at the ruling market price, which is quoted in loaves per man-hour.

In other words, the features of this model are as follows :

(1) No change in the effective limitational factors can occur.

(2) No change in the price of credit (money rate of interest) can affect the situation, since there is no credit.

(3) No change in factor substitution rates, i.e. relative prices of different factors, can occur, since there is only one factor.

(4) The only relevant type of change, given the basic technology depicted by the matrix, and the initial resources of the entrepreneur, is a change in price of output in terms of the price of input.

To depict the above situation we have drawn up Table 47.   This shows a long and a short method of production, each of which has a given physical productivity.   We may imagine that the long method takes one year, and the short method six months.   Table 47 also shows the activity of

[1] *Individualism and Economic Order*, p. 223.

		ACTIVITIES					RESOURCES
		PURCHASE OF LABOUR		PRODUCTION			
				SHORT		LONG	
		Period 1	Period 2	Period 1	Period 2		
		I	II	III	IV	V	
Intensities	$f<1$	100	0	0	0	$100f$	≥ -100
	$f>1$	100	$101f$	$100f$	$101f^2$	0	
Loaves Period 1		-1		-1		-1	> 0
Labour hrs. Period 1		f		$1\cdot01$			> 0
Loaves Period 2			-1		-1		> 0
Labour hrs. Period 2			f			f	
Profit (loaves)		0	0	0	$1\cdot01$	$1\cdot0201$	Max.

Figures give physical quantities.

Internal prices are expressed in terms of value of labour.

TABLE 47

Internal prices

$f<1$	$f>1$
$y_1 = f$	$y_1 = f$
$y_2 = 1$	$y_2 = 1$
$y_3 = \cdot99f$	$y_3 = \cdot99$
$y_4 = \cdot99$	$y_4 = \dfrac{\cdot99}{f}$
$y_5 = \cdot98$	$y_5 = \dfrac{\cdot98}{f}$

buying labour in the market, during each period. Since in the model we are considering the variable in the situation is the price of the output (bread) in terms of labour, this price is entered in the Table as f, not as a particular number. The initial resources of the entrepreneur, 100 loaves, are shown as a boundary condition in the Table.

The entrepreneur may use his limited resources to produce output quickly, or by the slower method. Which will maximize his profit? The answer depends upon the price of labour in terms of output, and the formulae expressing this dependence are simple. We shall simplify the problem a little by assuming that the entrepreneur does not have any preference for profits earned at different times within the year, so that he takes his profit at the end of the year. This means that profit earned at mid-year is necessarily ploughed back into production. The total profit that could be obtained by utilizing the 100 loaves which constitute the entrepreneur's initial resources to hire labour for the long process of production is: $100 \times 1 \cdot 0201 f$. Similarly the total profit which could be obtained by utilizing the 100 loaves to hire labour for the short process of production is $100 \times (1 \cdot 01)^2 f^2$.

We have chosen our figures such that, for the value $f = 1$, the total profit made during the year is equal for the long and the short processes. That is, we have chosen figures such that for $f = 1$ the lower profit per turnover in the short process is just compensated by the greater number of turnovers per year. It is at once evident from the formulae that if profit is made equal for the value $f = 1$, then for $f > 1$ the annual profit must be greater on the short process than on the long process. Conversely, for $f < 1$ the annual profit must be less on the short process than on the long process.[1] The meaning of this is that

[1] It is always possible to make the critical value unity by suitable choice of units.

we may imagine an initial state of equilibrium in which the relative price of labour in terms of output, and the relative physical productivities of long and short processes, are such that the entrepreneur can earn exactly the same profit by the end of the year whether he invests in long or short processes or a mixture of both. Then a fall in wages relative to output prices must increase the relative profitability of short processes more than it increases that of long ones. If, for instance, f changes from 1 to 1·1, denoting a 10 per cent fall in the price of labour in terms of output, then profit in the long process rises from 102·01 to 112·21, while profit in the short process rises from 102·01 to 123·43. Thus, supposing that initially when the annual profit rate was the same on long and short processes the entrepreneur had invested some of his resources in the long processes, the fall in wages must cause a shift to shorter processes. Conversely, a rise in wages must cause a shift to longer processes.[1] If, for instance, f changes from 1 to 0·9, denoting a 10 per cent rise in wages, profit in the long process falls to 91·81 while that in the short process falls to 82·63. This is the gist of Professor Hayek's reasoning in the first part of his article on 'The Ricardo Effect', when he is examining his problem under the abstraction of an economy without money.

A Two-Factor Firm in a World with Cash but no Credit

The model we have used so far is, as is very apparent from the summary of features of the model given on page 160, so highly simplified as to be of little interest. We have to broaden it so as to make it reflect, at least in principle, some more features of a real economy.

The first point that must now be clarified is this:

---

[1] Professor Hayek, *Individualism and Economic Order*, p. 223, note, seems to have had doubts about the reversibility of his argument. These must have arisen from a more complex model than our own. In the present example the rule — like Professor Hayek's arithmetic on page 227 — has to work in either direction.

A.A.—M

'Capital', in the last analysis, is not a measurable entity. It is the whole collection of non-permanent resources — a manifold bundle of things.[1]   Furthermore, it is not to be associated in any simple way with Time, or 'the period of production'.   For this reason we shall distinguish sharply between 'the length of processes of production' on the one hand, and the degree of mechanization or ratio of capital equipment to labour used in these processes, on the other. In what follows we shall assume that there are only two physical types of resource, labour and machines.   We shall use the term 'capital intensity' of a process to refer to the ratio of capital equipment to labour in any process of *given* duration.   The length of process will refer to the time between starting a productive activity and finishing it, in any process of given capital intensity.   In fact, we know that longer processes tend to be more highly mechanized.   But the two are not to be identified.   In the kind of short period dynamic reactions from which our present problems arise, the two things may not go together.   Some aspects of these problems arise from changing relative prices of the different factors of production;   others from the changing relative prices of factors of production as a whole, or input, in terms of the price of output.   For this reason it is a useful analytic device to divorce completely the 'length of processes' from the 'capital intensity of processes'.   Thus the model used below (Table 48) has twice as many production activities as were shown in Table 47, so that it may reflect both these features.[2]

[1] Hayek, *Pure Theory of Capital*, chap. vii.

[2] It is a moot point whether in models separating these two features the term 'capital' is best attached to the feature of mechanization or whether it should rather be used to denote long processes.   In these models 'machines' are quite parallel to labour in respect of both durability and indivisibility. The length of process, in the present models, is more directly linked to problems of the rate of interest than is the degree of mechanization.   However, the assigning of the term 'capital' to one or other of the analytically separate features which are commonly associated with the word 'capital' is ultimately a terminological matter.

As Professor Hayek says, by excluding credit and the money rate of interest we have 'avoided what will later become our main problem'. For the present we shall still continue to exclude these; however, as a first step towards a model which can deal with them we have, in Table 48, introduced cash. The economy is a monetary economy, in which factors and products may be exchanged against cash; but there is still no credit, and hence no rate of interest. The extension of the model to reflect cash sales requires an additional activity (IX) to represent cash sales of product at mid-year. The activities representing purchase of factors will show exchange of factors against cash (not against product as in our barter model). There is no need to tabulate the activities of factor purchase in the first period, since we are examining the position of an entrepreneur who owns initially only factors, not cash. Hence the possibility of buying factors can arise only in the second period.

As in Table 47, so also in Table 48 we have presented the model in the form of a numerical example, leaving unspecified only that particular variable the influence of whose variation we wish to examine. We are still concerned with the same problem: namely, the effect of changes in the relative price of the output upon production methods. However, the output price is now, in this monetary model, expressed directly as the cash price of output sold (not as the price of output in terms of factor, as in our barter model). This cash price is shown as 'p' in Activity IX of Table 48.

It is important to make clear that, when we use numerical examples to demonstrate general principles about the influence of changes in particular variables of the system, the actual coefficients obtained for the critical values of the parameters are arbitrary. Thus in the problem tabulated in Table 47, we pitched the figures so that the

ACTIVITIES | RESOURCES

Intensities / Internal Prices	I	II	III	IV	V	VI	VII	VIII	IX	RESOURCES
	PURCHASE OF FACTORS		PRODUCTION — SHORT				PRODUCTION — LONG		SALE OF OUTPUT	
	CAPITAL	LABOUR	CAPITAL INTENSIVE		LABOUR INTENSIVE		CAPITAL INTENSIVE	LABOUR INTENSIVE		
	Period 2	Period 2	Period 1	Period 2	Period 1	Period 2				
Intensities:										
$p<2\cdot4$	0	0	0	0	0	0	1	1	0	
$p=2\cdot4$*	84	396	1	1·2	1	1·2	0	0	200	
$p>2\cdot4$	$\frac{p}{2\cdot4}\times84$	$\frac{p}{2\cdot4}\times396$	1	$\frac{p}{2\cdot4}\times1\cdot2$	1	$\frac{p}{2\cdot4}\times1\cdot2$	0	0	200	
Internal Prices										
$y_1 = {\cdot}67$ — Machine hrs. Period 1			-25		-10		-25	-10		$\geqslant -35$
$y_2 = 1$ — Labour hrs. Period 1			-50		-60		-50	-60		$\geqslant -110$
$y_3 = {\cdot}67$ — Output Period 1			100		100				-1	$\geqslant 0$
$y_4 = \frac{{\cdot}67}{p}$ — Cash Period 2	-1	-1								$\geqslant 0$
$y_5 = \frac{1{\cdot}33}{p}$ — Machine hrs. Period 2	·5			-25		-10				$\geqslant 0$
$y_6 = \frac{2}{p}$ — Labour hrs. Period 2		·33		-50		-60				$\geqslant 0$
$y_7 = {\cdot}56\ (p<2\cdot4)$ or $\frac{1{\cdot}33}{p}\ (p>2\cdot4)$ — Profit (output)	0	0					0	0	p	Max.

* This assumes that only short processes are used. But any combination of the solution with only short processes and that with only the long process is optimal for $p=2\cdot4$.

entrepreneur earned the same profit on long and short processes when the price per unit output (in terms of labour) was unity. We then showed that as this price is raised above unity the short processes become relatively more profitable, and as it falls below unity the converse holds. The significance of this conclusion is that as the output price increases above some critical value, short processes become relatively more profitable, and as the output price falls below the critical value, the converse holds. The equating of this critical value to unity is not significant, it is arbitrary — as must indeed be obvious when we remember that the units to which the prices refer are themselves arbitrary. In Table 48 we have selected figures which make the critical value of the output price not unity, but 2·4. Any other value could equally well have been arrived at, by variations in the numerical figures chosen for factor prices and physical productivities.

One more incidental feature of Table 48 may be noted. The initial quantities of factors owned by the entrepreneur have been so chosen that unit level of activity in each of the processes (capital intensive and labour intensive) exactly exhausts them. The conclusion as to the influence of variations of output price upon the length of process used would, however, not be affected if the initial quantities of factors owned were changed. The present model still implicitly assumes that the entrepreneur's time-preference for consumption in period 1 as compared to that in period 2 is not sufficiently strong to cause him to take any of the surplus earned in period 1 for consumption. In other words, his time-preference is lower than the time rate of return in production. So long as this is true, time-preference can be omitted as it will not affect the solution to our problems. The features of this second model may then be summarized as follows:

(1) No change in the effective limitational factors can occur.

(2) No changes in the money rate of interest are relevant, since there is no credit.

(3) Changes in the prices of factors are relevant.

(4) Changes in the prices of output are relevant.

As before, to illustrate the working of the principle that a rise in output price relatively to factor prices raises the relative profitability of shorter processes, we choose as our starting-point a situation in which the profitability is the same on both processes. The return on the entrepreneur's factors in the long process is simply the physical output per year, which is given in the last row of Activities VII and VIII. It is 120. The return on his factors in the short process is the square of the physical output per half-year, multiplied by the price of the output in terms of cash divided by cash price of the average factor-bundle used in short processes.

Thus let physical product per year in long processes be π_2, let physical product per half-year in short processes be π_1, let cash price of output be p,
let cash price of average factor-bundle in short processes be q.

Then : profitability in long processes is π_2,

profitability in short processes is $\dfrac{\pi_1^2 p}{q}$.

With the figures chosen in Table 48 :

$$\pi_2 = 120$$
$$\pi_1 = 100$$
$$q = 200$$

$\therefore$ For $\pi_2 = \dfrac{\pi_1^2 p}{q}$, we must have $p = 2 \cdot 4$.

It is at once apparent that the profitability of short processes of production increases relatively to that of long ones, in proportion as p is increased above $2 \cdot 4$, other things remaining equal. Conversely, as p is reduced below $2 \cdot 4$, the profitability of long processes rises above that in short ones. This is the same result as was previously reached for a single-factor barter economy. Table 48 summarizes the solutions for allocation of resources, and for internal prices, for $p = 2 \cdot 4$, $p < 2 \cdot 4$, and $p > 2 \cdot 4$.

For $p = 2 \cdot 4$ the equilibrium allocation of resources is 'neutral' as between long and short processes of production. If all resources are put into the short processes (IV and VI) the total profit is 240. Equally, if all resources are put into long processes (VII and VIII) total profit is 240. Suppose now that p rises by 10 per cent. Then profits in the short process rise by 10 per cent, the levels of activity in IV and VI being increased from $1 \cdot 2$ to $1 \cdot 32$. Profit in the long process is unaffected by the change (since there are no mid-year sales of product) so that the profitability of short processes rises relatively as well as absolutely. The converse is true if output prices fall below $2 \cdot 4$, profitability in the short process falling proportionately.

The present model may also be used to illustrate the familiar proposition that a fall in the price of one factor, say labour, relatively to the other, say machines, will make it profitable to substitute labour-intensive for capital-intensive processes, other things equal. This may easily be seen by inserting different coefficients in the factor purchasing activities and following through the effects on the solution.

A Firm with Internal Resources and Limited Credit

We shall now pass to a third model. Here we suppose that the entrepreneur has certain resources of his own and also can borrow cash outside. That is, we introduce credit into the economy. We assume that the amount of cash he can borrow at a given rate of interest is *limited* (this model can be extended quite easily to cases where more credit can be had at a higher interest rate; but we shall suppose that only the first block of credit, available at a given interest rate, is relevant). Changes in factor prices and commodity prices still affect the equilibrium in the same way as under the earlier models. But three new features appear, namely:

(1) Changes in the price of credit (money rate of interest) may affect the situation.

(2) The factors which are effectively limitational may change, under price variations.

(3) Differences between substitution rates obtaining in producer's activities and those obtaining on the market may exist, and these may exercise a significant influence on the equilibrium reached after variations in relative prices.

This model is represented in Table 49. To simplify the exposition, variations in the period of production have now been excluded. The purchasing of factors in the market is, as before, depicted in the first two activities. But these factor-purchase activities now entail not only an input of current cash and an output of factors, but also an input of future cash equal to the initial cost of the factors, plus interest. This is because the purchase is made with borrowed money, which has to be paid back later, with interest.[1]

An entrepreneur situated in the position depicted in Table 49 may either produce with his own factors only, or he may take up the credit available to him and expand his operations by purchasing additional factors. His choice between these two courses will be determined by the rate

---

[1] At first sight the input of both current and future cash depicted in each factor purchasing activity might suggest that under this formulation the entrepreneur is being made to pay the principal back twice. This is, however, not so, for the input of current cash does not come from his own resources, but from credit available. It is shown in the boundary conditions.

of interest. At some levels the interest rate will be prohibitively high, so that the taking up of credit would involve loss. There will, in general, be some critical value of the interest rate at which the taking up of credit brings neither loss nor gain. This rate may be determined from the first two activities of Table 49. In order that borrowing should be profitable the (internal) valuation of the principal and interest to be paid back in Period 2 must be no greater than the (internal) valuation of the factors that may be bought with the loan. That is, borrowing involves a loss unless:

either $\qquad\qquad\quad\cdot 6y_2 \geqslant (1 + r)y_5$

or $\qquad\qquad\quad\cdot 45y_3 \geqslant (1 + r)y_5.$

The equilibrium values of the y's for our example are given in Table 49. It will be seen there that $y_2 = \cdot 67$ and $y_3 = 1$, so that $\cdot 45y_3 > \cdot 6y_2$. Therefore, the relevant condition for absence of loss from borrowing is $\cdot 45y_3 \geqslant (1 + r)y_5$. That is, since the equilibrium value of y_5 is $\cdot 411$, $r \leqslant 8$ per cent. For all values of r below 8 per cent borrowing is profitable, for values above it borrowing involves loss. If no credit is taken up, and production proceeds purely by the utilization of the 35 owned machines and the 110 owned units of labour, then with the figures in Table 49 total production, which is equal to total consumption, is 200 units of product. This may be computed by putting

$$25x_3 + 10x_4 = 35$$
$$50x_3 + 60x_4 = 110,$$

which gives $x_3 = x_4 = 1$, for the levels of activity in production Activities III and IV, each of which gives 100 units of product at unit level.

If credit is taken up the producer will find it profitable, on the figures chosen, to buy labour only. This is because

ACTIVITIES

	I Machines	II Labour	III Capital Intensive	IV Labour Intensive	V Sale	VI Consumption	Resources
	Purchase of Factors		**Production**		**Sale**	**Consumption**	
Intensities $r>8\%$	0	0	1	1	0	200	
$r<8\%$	0	200	·1	3·25	$\dfrac{200(1+r)}{1\cdot 6}$	$335 - x_5$	
Cash (in £) Period 1	-1	-1					$\geqslant -200$
Machine hrs. Period 1	·6		-25	-10			$\geqslant -35$
Labour hrs. Period 1		·45	-50	-60			$\geqslant -110$
Output Period 1			100	100	-1	-1	$\geqslant 0$
Cash (in £) Period 2	$-(1+r)$	$-(1+r)$			1·6		$\geqslant 0$
Profit (output)	0	0	0	0	0	1	Max.

Internal prices

$y_1 = ·45 - (1+r)y_5$ *   Cash (in £) Period 1
$y_2 = ·67$ Machine hrs. Period 1
$y_3 \equiv 1$ Labour hrs. Period 1
$y_4 = ·67$ Output Period 1
$y_5 = ·417$ Cash (in £) Period 2
$y_6 = ·67$ Profit (output)

* For $r>8\%$ $y_1=0$. All other y values are the same for $r>8\%$ and $r<8\%$.

Figures give physical quantities. Internal prices are expressed in terms of value of labour. x_5 is intensity in Activity V.

TABLE 49

the market price of labour, relative to the price of machinery, is lower than labour's value (relative to that of machinery) in his existing operations with his owned resources. We shall revert to this point later on. By devoting the £200 available credit resources to the purchase of additional labour costing $£\frac{20}{9}$ per unit, the entrepreneur increases his productive resources by 90 labour units, so that he has 200 units of labour with 35 units of machinery. The levels of activity in the production activities are then solved from the equations

$$25x_3 + 10x_4 = 35$$
$$50x_3 + 60x_4 = 200,$$

yielding $x_3 = \cdot 1$ and $x_4 = 3\cdot25$. Total production when credit is utilized is therefore 335 units, that is 135 more than can be produced without taking up the available credit. Thus using £200 credit gives a gross return of 135 units of output, which is $135p$ units of cash (£s). At the same time the using of £200 credit involves costs of £200 $(1 + r)$. Hence borrowing involves a loss unless $135p \geqslant 200\ (1 + r)$ i.e. $r \leqslant \frac{135}{200}\ p - 1$. Inserting the particular value of $p = 1\cdot6$ used in Table 49, we get again $r \leqslant 8$ per cent as the critical value at which borrowing becomes profitable. This critical value is here determined by reference to the quantity of cash coming in, and the quantity going out as a result of borrowing. Looked at from this aspect the critical condition is expressed as $135p \geqslant 200\ (1 + r)$. We previously determined the critical value by considering the dual aspect — the valuations of the factors purchasable with credit on the one hand, and of the loan repayment on the other. This was expressed in the condition $\cdot45y_3 \geqslant (1 + r)y_5$. Substituting the particular values used in our example, $p = 1\cdot6$, $y_3 = 1$, $y_5 = \cdot416$, the two conditions are seen to yield the same critical value, $r \leqslant 8$ per cent. The numerical solutions for levels of intensities, as well as the dual solution for internal values, for the cases where $r > 8$ per cent and $r < 8$ per cent respectively, are listed in Table 49.

We wish now to revert to a feature of the particular numerical example we are using, to which attention was drawn on p. 173 above. As may be seen by consulting Table 49, the internal value of labour in relation to that of machinery, when the producer uses nothing but his own resources, does not coincide with the postulated market prices. Internally, one unit of labour is worth $1\frac{1}{2}$ machines. On the market one unit of labour is worth only $1\frac{1}{3}$ machines. So long as the rate of interest remains so high as to preclude borrowing, this discrepancy has no repercussion on the equilibrium position. If, however, the money rate of interest drops to a level at which it is profitable to take up credit and produce with hired factors, the market prices of the latter become one of the factors determining the equilibrium. If these market prices are the same as the relative productivities of the factors in the activities conducted with the entrepreneur's own resources, then the method of production used in activities conducted with hired resources must be the same as that used when activities were conducted solely with owned resources. If, however, the market prices of factors diverge from their relative productivities in the existing factory, this need not be so. For instance, if the market price of labour in terms of machinery is lower than the relative productivity of labour compared with machinery in the existing factory, the consequence of the fall in the rate of interest from above to below the critical level will be to make the entrepreneur switch to more labour-intensive methods of production. This effect results from the passage from factor-limitation to credit-limitation as the effective limitation on activities. Before the fall in the money rate of interest the entrepreneur was effectively limited by the supply of his factors. If there were no change in the effectively limitational factors, there would be no alteration in the type of method used. Further, if the entry of credit as an effective limiting factor were not accompanied by a divergence between external and internal factor substitution rates, there would still be no alteration in the type of method used. But, to repeat, if the money rate of interest falls from above to below the critical value at which the taking up of available credit becomes profitable, then in a situation where the market price of labour in terms of machinery is less than the internal rate prevailing in the existing factory, it may pay the entrepreneur to concentrate all his newly financed activities upon labour-intensive processes, instead of using part of them upon capitalistic ones as before.

A quite similar reaction may result from a rise in commodity prices, instead of a fall in the money rate of interest. Under increased commodity prices the taking up of credit, previously unprofitable, may become profitable, and in similar conditions regarding external and internal factor substitution rates, a similar conclusion will be reached.

The above analysis is not limited to the particular case incorporated in the tables, where the amount of credit available is absolutely fixed. There can be any amount of credit available to the entrepreneur, provided only that the amount available *at a given rate of interest* is fixed. We could expand Table 49 to incorporate any number of successive credit *tranches*, available at successively higher interest rates, without essentially altering the reasoning. In other words, the analysis depends upon a rising supply schedule for credit, represented in our formulation as a step function. The effects of a fall in the rate of interest 'from above to below the critical value at which the taking up of available credit becomes profitable' are to be understood to follow whenever the rate of interest falls sufficiently to make profitable the utilization of an additional *tranche* of credit.

One feature which is essential to the above analysis is credit rationing. This divorces the money rate of interest from time-productivity in production and introduces the possibility — over certain finite ranges of variation — of changes in effective limitational factors. In order to arrive at the 'perverse' result of reduced demand for capital goods consequent upon a fall in the money rate of interest we must also postulate the existence of fixed internal resources of the entrepreneur (the use of which is costless, since any payment to them is already contracted for and it is assumed that they cannot be sold). This divorces internal factor substitution rates from market prices of factors. If these two diverge in the manner indicated above, changes in relative prices (including the price of money) may cause a shift to more labour-intensive processes in 'boom' conditions.

We have completed the examination of the repercussions upon production methods of any 'critical' fall in the rate of interest — that is, of any fall which renders a new *tranche* of credit profitable to the entrepreneur. We might also enquire what are the effects of a fall in the interest rate which is not sufficient to render new loans profitable.

In the conditions envisaged here, entrepreneurs may be utilizing a limited volume of credit which they have been able to take up at a lower interest rate, even though they cannot get more credit at that rate. A general fall in the structure of interest rates will affect the profitability of the operations based on this credit. The line of reasoning frequently applied in this context is that a reduction in money interest induces an increase in the amount of credit used and factors bought. With 'infinite elasticities of supply' of all these things, there would be a general expansion of activity of all kinds, and no reason for any change in the entrepreneur's pattern of activities. But here we assume that no more credit is forthcoming when the rate of interest charged on credit is reduced. Hence activities cannot expand. However, the lower money interest charge is really a fall in cost of input, in terms of price of output. In other words, it may act like the rise in commodity prices compared to factor costs examined above. What is no longer required for interest payment is freed for use in production, and this adds *more* profit by the end of the year if used in the short process than it would if used in the long process. This possibility arises because of our assumption of inelastic credit supply. It should be emphasized that the magnitude of this reaction is relatively small, since it operates only in respect of a minor element in costs, namely, interest payment.

The 'paradox' established here is to be understood if the nature of the situation is understood. Three different kinds of interest rate must be distinguished :

(1) The subjective time-discount for profits received at different periods.

(2) The physical time-productivity or growth through time, i.e. productivity of longer process compared to shorter.

(3) The charge made on credit or money rate of interest.

The two first factors are 'real'. They are the (Fisherian) concept of time-preference and the (Böhm-Bawerk) 'productivity of roundabout processes' respectively ; and they exist in a barter economy independently of money. In a dynamic world (commonly thought of as a 'disequilibrium situation') they need not equal the money rate, and they need not necessarily equal each other (e.g. we may constrain the time-distribution of output in any way we like, not to correspond with time-productivity.

Or we may put time-discount at nil, and time-productivity positive as, for instance, in Table 47). The above apparent paradox does not conflict with the common-sense point that a reduction of subjective time-preference tends to *increase* the length of process used (it is easy to construct a model where this element is allowed play, to demonstrate this). Again, the influence of changes in the monetary rate of interest must not be confused with the influence of changes in time-productivity. If the latter is reduced profits must fall (not rise, as when money rate falls). But we are here concerned neither with changes in technology nor with changes in time-preference; we are concerned with changes in the money rate of interest. Under the circumstances envisaged, a fall in the money rate represents a fall in the price of input in terms of output and it may, therefore, shorten the productive processes used.

In our models we have sharply distinguished between 'length of process' and 'capital intensity of process'. They are quite dissociated properties in our tables. It seemed important to dissociate them explicitly, since the two things are not identical and not *necessarily* correlated: the effects of changes in money rate of interest bear upon the length of process, but not necessarily upon the degree of labour intensiveness. On the other hand, the effects of changes in the ratio of wages to machine prices bear upon the degree of labour-intensiveness but not necessarily upon the length of process. (Professor Hayek does not always make it quite clear which feature he refers to, and this renders some of his passages obscure.) However, *in fact* there is some reason to suppose that as a general rule technology is such that a process which is shorter is likely to be less capitalistic. In so far as this is true, Professor Hayek's proof, which we examined earlier on, that a rise in commodity prices compared to factor costs causes a shift to shorter processes will entail also a relative decline in demand for capital goods, and even an absolute decline at current capital good prices.

Conclusion

Mathematical readers would probably have preferred a more rigorous formulation than that given in our Tables 47-49. These are in certain respects special cases, rather than general formulations. For each problem we have set up a different table of activities, making different simplifying assumptions and using specific figures for variables other than those whose influence is under consideration. A more general formulation would doubtless be more satisfying. One should incorporate all the main features simultaneously : an economic unit with credit, labour and machinery, able to produce by long or short processes, each of which may be either capital-intensive or labour-intensive ; and also able to borrow (or pay for purchased factors) for short or long periods, independently of the length of period adopted in production activities. The general model should allow for factors to be either fully utilized or partly idle ; and all possible relevant relationships between internal prices and market prices should be considered. The great complexity of such a formulation has driven us to resort here, as in other parts of this book, to the construction of a series of particular cases. What significance can then be attached to the results we have obtained ?

So far as concerns the artificial isolation of certain elements in the situation confronting the entrepreneur, such as is effected in Tables 47, 48, and 49 respectively, and the resort to numerical examples with only one figure varying parametrically, this procedure appears to be inelegant but not without significance. The tendencies towards particular kinds of change which we have established for these simple models and particular magnitudes would be at work in the postulated conditions in a more complete model. Whether or not any one of these particular tendencies would, in the complete model, have an important effect upon the outcome in which we are interested (length of process used; amount of credit taken up, etc.) is, of course, a question which could only be answered for a completely specified problem. But the forces identified in the simpler models would still be present in a more complex one reflecting simultaneously the different features referred to above. The question of whether or not this kind of analysis can give significant indications of the way in which a whole economy will develop through time raises, however, broader methodological issues. The arguments we have been examining and the models we have used refer to individual enterprises operating in an open economy — factors are bought, products sold, and credit obtained from outside the enterprise. The treatment is not a dynamic one, but rather that of comparative statics. If one wishes to assert that the reactions of individual entrepreneurs in the particular circumstances reviewed above determine the course of development of the economy through time, one has to be willing to take a great deal for granted. Consider, for instance, Professor Hayek's demonstration that a rise of commodity prices in terms of real wages tends to induce entrepreneurs to adopt shorter production processes. Is there any reason why the internal value of labour should tend to rise above its market price in a boom ? Is it either inevitable or probable that the market wage of labour will lag behind its value in production ? As for inevitability, Professor Hayek seems to yield the point that his main arguments do not establish this for the economy,[1] since at the end of his article he suggests a quite different order of

---

[1] *Individualism and Economic Order*, pp. 249-51.

reasons for the result — notably, that entrepreneurs will want 'to make hay while the sun shines', thereby bringing the explanation down to expectations. As for probability, no pronouncement will be made here as to how far and in what conditions actual technology, actual entrepreneur expectations, etc., etc., give rise to a presumption that the time-sequence of events will be as supposed in Professor Hayek's article. The models set out above show only that if this time-sequence prevails, Professor Hayek's results, other things equal, will follow. This is surely about as much as could be said of most theories of dynamic development in economics.

GEOMETRICAL APPENDIX TO CHAPTER IX

1. *Relation between the Joint Production Boundary and the Sum of the Separate Production Boundaries of Two Areas (Fig. A).*

Under the conditions discussed in Chapter IX, where there are two factors of production and identical techniques in two areas, the production boundaries show only two slopes. Both slopes occur on each area boundary. Fig. A reproduces Fig. 5 from Chapter IX. For convenience the point P_2 has been relabelled Q_I. Here the

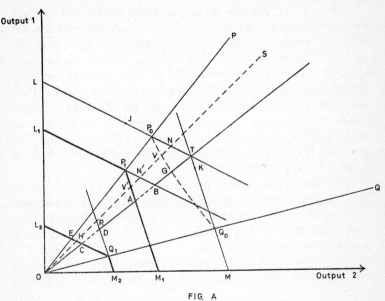

FIG. A

separate area boundaries are $L_IP_IM_I$ and $L_2Q_IM_2$. The joint production boundary may be viewed as the sum of the line segments L_IP_I and L_2Q_I, both having the flatter slope, and the sum of the line segments P_IM_I and Q_IM_2, both having the steeper slope. (Unless OP_I and OQ_I coincide, the kink of the joint boundary (T) thus formed must lie on a radial through the origin which is different from the radials upon which P_I and Q_I lie, and comes between them.) We then have $L_I P_I = LJ$; $L_2 E = JP_0$; $EQ_I = P_0 T$; $P_I M_I = KM$ and $Q_I M_2 = TK$.

For patterns of output above OP and below OQ the co-ordinates of the joint boundary are simply the sum of the co-ordinates of the two separate boundaries. For patterns between OP and OQ the former exceeds the latter. Thus consider any radial, say OS, between OP and OT. As may be proved, the intercept (N′N) cut off on this radial by the parallel lines LT and $L_I P_I$ produced, equals the intercept OH cut off on it by Area II's boundary. That is, NN′ equals separate production in Area II. The remaining part of the joint production (ON′) exceeds Area I's separate production (OV′) by V′N′. For patterns of production between OP and OT the gains from specialization are therefore marked off on the radials by the two lines $P_I A$ and $P_I B$.

Similarly for patterns of output between OT and OQ the intercept of any radial (e.g. one drawn through OK) which is cut off by the parallel lines MT and $M_I P_I$ exceeds the separate output of Area II by the length of this radial lying between the two lines $Q_I C$ and $Q_I D$, which is drawn parallel to MT; while the remaining part of joint output just equals the separate output of Area I. Thus the two triangles $P_I AB$ and $Q_I CD$ serve to mark off, on the respective radials, the amount of the excess of joint production over the sum of the isolated production in Area I and Area II respectively. For the radial OT the gain is shown both by AB and by CD, which are equal (OD = AT and OC = BT).

The sum of the isolated production in Area I and in Area II may be plotted, for output patterns between OP and OQ, by subtracting from the joint boundary the excess amounts established above. This yields the boundary $P_0 VGQ_0$. It may be proven that this is a curve convex to the origin.

The construction used in Fig. 6 depicting indifference loci for two consumers is similar, *mutatis mutandis*. Here $P_0 NT_0$ and $T_0 MQ_0$ are curved.

2. *Influence of Factor Endowment Ratio on the Gain from Specialization (Fig. B).*

Fig. B depicts the production of two outputs in two areas, using two factors of production.

Assume a *given* total production possibility boundary for the areas taken together, indicated by LTM (Fig. B). Assume further a *given* factor endowment ratio for one of the areas, say Area I. For given technical coefficients of production this ratio may be indicated by drawing a radial through the origin, OP, upon which the kink of the production boundary for Area I must fall. The point where it falls is not assumed given, but varies with the size of Area I's resources.

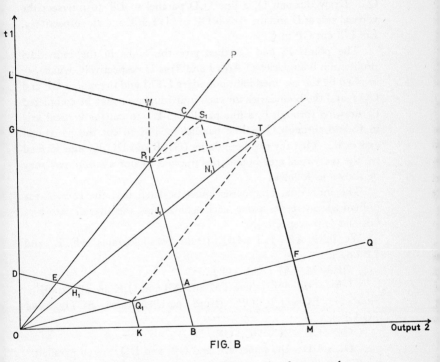

FIG. B

Let the corresponding radial indicating the factor endowment ratio in Area II be a variable. It may vary between the horizontal axis and the radial OT, as the relative sizes of the resources of Area I and Area II vary.

Prove: that the gain from trade is greater the greater the angle POQ where OQ indicates the radial resulting from the factor endowment ratio in Area II.

Proof: For a given total production possibility boundary (LTM) and a given ratio of factor endowment (resulting in a given radial OP) in Area I, the individual production possibility boundaries for each area may be constructed *for each specified factor endowment ratio in Area II*, as follows :

Assume the factor endowment ratio in Area II is indicated by OQ. Draw through T a line TP_I parallel to OQ, and intersecting OP at P_I. From P_I draw P_IB parallel to TM to intersect OQ at A and OM at B and OT at J_I. Let TM cut OQ in F.

Draw through T a line TQ_I parallel to OP to intersect OQ at Q_I. Draw through Q_I a line Q_ID parallel to LT to intersect the vertical axis at D and the radials OP and OT at E and H_I respectively. Let LT cut OP in C.

The points P_I and Q_I then give the kinks in the individual production boundaries of Area I and Area II respectively, which are implied by the assumed joint boundary LTM and the radials OP and OQ ; and the boundaries for each individual area may be completed by drawing through P_I a line parallel to LT to cut the vertical axis in G and through Q_I a line parallel to TM to cut the horizontal axis in K. That the two boundaries (GP_IB and DQ_IK) thus formed are the individual area boundaries implied by our assumptions may be shown as follows :

The individual boundaries must be such that the sum of the individual intercepts along each axis equals the overall intercept OL and OM respectively.

We have $AF = P_IT = OQ_I$ (from parallelograms $AFTP_I$ and TP_IOQ_I).

$\therefore OF = OA + AF = OA + OQ_I$.

$\therefore OM = OB + OK$ (since TM and AB and Q_IK are all parallel). Similarly, $EC = Q_IT = OP_I$ (from parallelograms $ECTQ_I$ and TQ_IOP_I).

$\therefore OC = OE + EC = OE + OP_I$.

$\therefore OL = OD + OG$ (since LC and GP_I and DQ_I are all parallel).

We have next to give the geometrical demonstration of the gain from international specialization, and to do this we must postulate consumption conditions. We shall assume that the pattern of consumption is fixed at the ratio indicated by the radial OT, though the argument may be extended to other given patterns of consumption. The gain from trade for any given pair of individual production boundaries, say GP_IB and DQ_IK, is found as follows : through P_I draw P_IS_I parallel to the radial OT to intersect CT in S_I. Draw S_IN_I parallel to TM to cut OT (the consumption radial) in N_I.

Then the total output of the two areas operating in isolation is ON_I. For production in the larger area is OJ_I and that in the smaller area is OH_I. But triangles OEH_I and P_ICS_I are identical (since $OE = P_IC$; $E\widehat{O}H_I = C\widehat{P}_IS_I$ and $O\widehat{E}H_I = P_I\widehat{C}S_I$). Therefore $OH_I = P_IS_I$. But $P_IS_I = J_IN_I$, since $P_IS_IN_IJ_I$ is a parallelogram. Therefore the sum of the separate outputs of Areas I and II is $OJ_I + J_IN_I = ON_I$. The total output of the two areas operating jointly is OT. Thus the gain from trade is measured by the distance between N_I and T.

We have therefore to prove that N_IT increases as the angle POQ increases. For clarity, the necessary parts of Fig. B have been reproduced in Fig. C. We here show two positions for the lower radial, OQ and OQ'. Correspondingly, there are two positions for Area I's boundary kink on radial OP: the position P_I is the kink if OQ is the lower radial; the position P'_I is the kink if OQ' is the lower radial. As before, we draw P_IS_I parallel to OT to cut LT in S_I. We also draw $P'_IS'_I$ parallel to OT to cut CT in S'_I. Again S_IN_I is drawn parallel to TM to cut OT in N_I, and $S'_IN'_I$ is drawn parallel to TM to cut OT in N'_I.

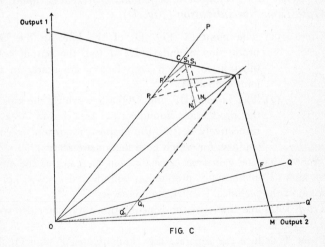

FIG. C

In the triangles OP_IT and OP'_IT, with one side and one angle in common, we have

$$OP_I < OP'_I \text{ since } P_I\widehat{T}O = T\widehat{O}Q < P'_I\widehat{T}O = T\widehat{O}Q'.$$

Subtracting this inequality from $CO = CO$, we have

$$CP'_I < CP_I.$$

Hence in the triangles $P_I S_I C$ and $P'_I S'_I C$ (which are similar) we have

$$CS'_I < CS_I.$$

Subtracting this inequality from $CT = CT$, we have

$$TS'_I > TS_I.$$

Thus in the triangles $TS'_I N'_I$ and $TS_I N_I$ (which are similar) we have

$$N'_I T > N_I T$$

which proves that as the angle TOQ increases, the gain from trade increases. That is, since the angle POT is given, as the angle POQ increases the gain from trade increases.

A similar technique may be used in connection with Fig. 6 to show that specialization in consumption brings more gain, for a given joint consumption boundary and given individual consumer substitution rates, the greater the angle POQ in Fig. 6.

3. *Influence of Technical Coefficient Differences upon the Gain from Specialization (Fig. D).*

Given : (1) The point (T Fig. D) of the kink in the joint production boundary LTM (i.e. the output combination for which both factors are scarce in the joint economy).

(2) The radials (OP and OQ) upon which the kink in the production boundary of Area I and Area II respectively lie (i.e. the output proportion, in each country, for which both factors are scarce).

Prove : that the gain from specialization increases as the angle at the kink (T) of the joint production boundary decreases, i.e. as variation of the technical coefficients increases.

Proof : Assume first that the consumption ratio coincides with the radial OT.

From T deduce the separate area kink points, P_I and Q_I, by drawing TP_I parallel to OQ to cut OP in P_I, and TQ_I parallel to OP to cut OQ in Q_I (as in § 2).

Draw $P_I S_I$ parallel to OT to cut LT in S_I.

Form a parallelogram $P_I S_I TK$ by drawing $P_I K$ parallel to $S_I T$.

Draw $Q_I H_I$ parallel to LT to cut OT in H_I.

Draw $P_I J_I$ parallel to MT to cut OT in J_I.

From the parallelogram $P_I T Q_I O$, $\triangle O P_I K = \triangle T Q_I H_I$ and $OK = H_I T$. Hence $OH_I = KT$.

Given the consumption ratio represented by OT, the individual areas' equilibrium outputs without trade are given by the intersection of their production boundaries with OT. That is, the sum of the outputs with no trade is $OJ_I + OH_I$

$$= OJ_I + KT.$$

Now, as the angle at T approaches the maximum of $180°$ (and M approaches M') J_I approaches K and the sum of outputs with no trade approaches $OK + KT = OT$, which is the output with specialization. Thus, since $\widehat{MTM'} = \widehat{J_I P_I K}$, as the former approaches 0 the latter also approaches 0 and therefore $J_I K$, which measures the gain from trade, approaches 0.

A similar construction may be applied for any variation in the angle LTM, whether LT and MT are both varied simultaneously, or singly.

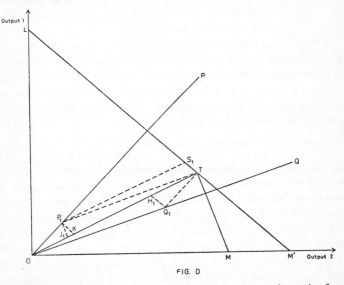

FIG. D

In general, for any given consumption pattern the gain from specialization will be measured by the segment on the consumption radial which is marked off by the pair of lines, with the slopes of LT and MT respectively, drawn through *either* P_I *or* Q_I, whichever gives the smaller segment. Apart from this complication the construction is the same as before. Hence : for any consumption pattern the gain from specialization is larger the smaller the angle LTM.

A similar technique may be used to show that specialization in consumption offers more gain the greater the difference in the slopes of the two consumer indifference loci, other things being equal.

4. *Influence of the Relative Size of the two Areas upon the Gain from Specialization (Fig. E).*

Given : (1) The radials (OP and OQ) upon which the kinks in the production boundary of Area I and Area II respectively lie.

(2) The slopes of the production boundaries.

(3) The total output of the two areas producing *separately*, in terms of any given consumption bundle of the two outputs.

Prove : that the gain from specialization is greater the more nearly the relative size of the two areas approaches the 'optimum'. In other words, define the optimum relative size for the two areas.

Proof : Assume that the consumption ratio is that depicted along OR (Fig. E) and that the fixed total output of the two areas acting in isolation is given by the point N.

Suppose first that the ratio of the $\dfrac{\text{size of Area I}}{\text{size of Area II}}$ is infinite, that is, that Area I produces the whole of the output at N, and Area II produces nothing. In this case the point N represents the intersection of Area I's production boundary with the radial OR. Thus the kink of Area I's boundary must be at the intersection, P_0, of OP with a line drawn through N having the steeper of the given production boundary slopes. The sum of the isolated production of the two areas is simply that of Area I, and is identical with the total output under 'joint' production. The joint production boundary is $L_0 P_0 M_0$.

Now let Area I decline a little in size — say to P_1, giving the output OJ_1 for the consumption ratio assumed. Area II must therefore expand from zero output to give an output of $J_1 N$. Construct $OH_1 = J_1 N$. This implies that Area II's boundary runs along the line $E_IH_IQ_I$ with the slope of L_IT_I. That is, Area II's boundary kink is at Q_I.

Thus (by the inverse of the construction used in § 2) the joint production boundary kink lies at the intersection (T_I) of the line (P_IT_I) drawn through P_I parallel to OQ, with a line drawn through Q_I parallel to OP. Thus, when the two areas have the sizes indicated by the outputs OH_I and OJ_I respectively, the joint boundary has its kink at T_I; and the joint boundary runs along L_IT_I (parallel to L_0P_0) and T_IM_I (parallel to NM_0). The equilibrium joint output is therefore given by the point of intersection between this joint boundary and the consumption radial (point G in Fig. E).

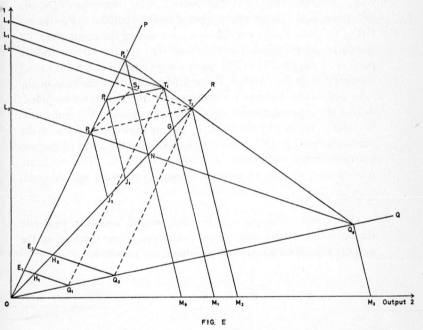

FIG. E

The gain from specialization, when the two areas have isolated outputs OJ_I and OH_I, is seen to be given by the intercept NG (the difference between joint output OG and the sum of the isolated outputs, ON).

For what relative sizes of the two areas is NG maximized? Our problem is to consider how the position of T, and hence of G, varies as the ratio $\dfrac{\text{size of Area I}}{\text{size of Area II}}$ varies. We have seen that if this ratio is infinite then T is at the point of intersection, P_0, of OP with the line NP_0, this line being drawn through the fixed point N and having the steeper of the two given production boundary slopes. Similarly, if the ratio $\dfrac{\text{size of Area I}}{\text{size of Area II}}$ is zero, signifying that all production comes from Area II, T is at the intersection, Q_0, of OQ with the line NQ_0, this line being drawn through the fixed point N and having the flatter of the two given production boundary slopes.

Now it may be proved that, given the fixed point N, the locus of the kink T of the joint production boundary is the line P_0Q_0. Further, the slope of this line lies between that of P_0N and that of NQ_0. Let P_0Q_0 cut OR in T_2. Since P_0Q_0 is flatter than P_0N, any line — say T_1G — drawn from a point on P_0T_2 parallel to P_0N to cut OR in G, must always cut OR at a point nearer the origin than T_2. Similarly, since P_0Q_0 is steeper than NQ_0, any line drawn from a point on T_2Q_0 parallel to NQ_0 must always cut OR at a point nearer the origin than T_2. Hence T_2 itself (denoting that the kink of the joint production boundary coincides with the consumption radial) defines the optimal relative sizes of the two Areas. The individual boundaries implied by the point T_2 may be drawn in by forming the parallelogram $T_2P_2OQ_2$, where P_2 and Q_2 give the kinks of the two individual area boundaries, as explained in § 2. The optimum relative size, or ratio of isolated outputs, for Area I and Area II, is given by $\dfrac{OJ_2}{OH_2}$.

The above technique may be used, *mutatis mutandis*, to define the optimum relative size of two consumers, given the total of the outputs consumed when each consumer acts in isolation.

REFERENCES

R. G. D. ALLEN. *Mathematical Economics*. Macmillan. 1956.

A. CHARNES, W. W. COOPER, and A. M. HENDERSON. *An Introduction to Linear Programming*. Wiley, New York. 1953.

J. CHIPMAN. 'Linear Programming', *Review of Economics and Statistics*, May 1953.

R. DORFMAN. *Application of Linear Programming to the Theory of the Firm*. University of California. 1951.

R. DORFMAN. 'Mathematical or "Linear" Programming : A Non-mathematical Exposition', *American Economic Review*, December 1953.

T. C. KOOPMANS (Ed.). *Activity Analysis of Production and Allocation*. Wiley, New York ; Chapman & Hall, London. 1951.

T. C. KOOPMANS. 'Maximization and Substitution in Linear Models of Production.' *Input-Output Relations. Proceedings of a Conference on Inter-Industrial Relations* held at Driebergen, Holland, by the Netherlands Economic Institute. H. E. Stentfert-Kroese. N. V. Leyden. 1953.

T. C. KOOPMANS. 'Optimum Utilization of the Transport System', *Econometrica*, July 1949. Supplement.

G. MORTON. 'Notes on Linear Programming', *Economica*, November 1951.

P. NEWMAN. 'Some Calculations on Least-Cost Diets using the Simplex Method', *Bulletin of the Oxford University Institute of Statistics*, August 1955.

THE END

PRINTED BY R. & R. CLARK, LTD., EDINBURGH